Distinctive Serger
Gifts and Crafts

Distinctive Serger Gifts and Crafts

An Idea Book for All Occasions

Naomi Baker and Tammy Young

Chilton Book Company
Radnor, Pennsylvania

Copyright © 1989 by Naomi Baker and
Tammy Young
All Rights Reserved
Published in Radnor, Pennsylvania
19089, by Chilton Book Company

Color Photographs by Lee Phillips
Book Design by Martha Vercoutere
Cover and Color Pages designed
by Kevin Culver
Illustrations by Chris Hansen
Samples Sewn by Naomi Baker

Manufactured in the United States of
America

Library of Congress Cataloging in
Publication Data

Baker, Naomi.
    Distinctive serger gifts & crafts: an
    idea book for all occasions/Naomi
    Baker and Tammy Young.

    p. cm.—(Creative machine arts
    series)
    IBSN 0-8019-7985-4 :
    1. Serging. 2. Machine sewing.
    I. Young, Tammy. II. Title.
III. Title: Distinctive serger gifts and
crafts. IV. Series.
TT713.B33 1989   89-42852
646.2'044—dc20   CIP

Contents

Preface

It's been exciting writing an entire book specifically on serged gifts and crafts. There were several reasons why we chose to do so:

As managing editor of the *Serger Update* newsletter, Tammy has received numerous requests for more information on the subject. And Naomi, who writes extensively on serging techniques, has recognized a void of information here as well.

As we began to include more gift and craft projects in our serger periodicals, we recognized the potential for even greater creativity. Duplicating expensive items that we saw in retail stores or in mail-order catalogs was fun and rewarding. And, of course, those who have received our special gifts appreciated the personal touch.

In assembling the book, we included in every chapter projects with varying levels of difficulty. The first projects will be the easiest and generally the fastest. As you proceed through each chapter, projects become more difficult and time-consuming.

Throughout the book, we have assumed that you know how to set your serger for a balanced-tension seam or edge finish, so we have not included those instructions. Your manual or your local dealer can help you with any problems in these areas. We also assume that you know other serger basics. For further clarification, we have included a glossary of serger-specific terms and techniques we use. For more information on basic serger sewing, also see your local dealer.

Although we include simple projects throughout the book, we have tried to stretch our creativity to give you projects that incorporate most of the new serger techniques we've developed recently, such as: serged lace and serged wires, serged scalloped edges, double rolled-edge braid and binding, serging padded paper, mock hemstitching, serger quilting, serged piping and couching, and much more.

You will already have many needed supplies on hand. We have listed any recommended specialty threads under "Materials Needed," but assume you will have all-purpose or serger thread available for each project, too. Any specific supplies that are difficult to find locally can be purchased through mail-order companies. For a listing, write *Serger Update* at the address listed on page ii.

Sergers have captivated those of us who love sewing. New techniques, embellishment, finishing, and, ultimately, never-before-possible projects are now a special challenge. We hope you'll have as much serging fun exploring these possibilities as we have and then move ahead to creative successes of your own.

Naomi Baker and Tammy Young

Acknowledgments

Sincere thanks to our super-creative serger-sewing friends who have helped develop ideas for this book: Gail Brown, Barb Griffin, Nancy Nix Rice, Sue Green, Nancy Kores, Janet Klaer, Jan Saunders, and Virginia Fulcher.

Also invaluable to the completion of this book were the major machine companies and their local dealers who have given us ongoing support, information, and inspiration. Our thanks to these firms, listed in alphabetical order and paired with their respective serger brand names (in parentheses): Bernina of America (Bernette and FunLock), Brother International Corp. (Homelock), Elna, Inc. (Elnalock and Elnita), Fabri-Centers of America (Toyota), Juki Industries of America (Juki Lock), New Home Sewing Machine Co. (MyLock and Combi), Pfaff American Sales (Hobbylock), Riccar America (Riccar Lock), Simplicity Sewing Machines (Easy Lock), Singer Sewing Machine Co. (Ultralock), Tacony Corp. (Baby Lock and Serge-Mate), Viking Sewing Machine Co. (Huskylock), and White Sewing Machine Co. (Superlocks).

In addition, a very special thank you to two members of the Serger Update newsletter staff without whom this book could not have been completed: first, to our hard-working assistant editor, Lori Bottom, for her diligent efforts in preparing the manuscript; and also to our talented illustrator, Chris Hansen, who helps us clarify every technique.

1. Housewarming Party

Special Gift Bags

Three fancy little bags will wrap up a variety of gifts for a housewarming party and other occasions, too. Decorate them with your serger for a personal touch, then fill with a package of Russian tea, a favorite bottle of wine, or potpourri.

Fig. 1-1

Fig. 1-2

Quilted Tea Bag
With Reversible-Edge Binding and Serger Braid Tie

Materials Needed
• **Fabric:** 1/4 yard of 45"-wide, double-faced quilted fabric (for three bags).

• **Heavy thread:** One spool, cone, or ball of pearl cotton, crochet thread, or buttonhole twist.

Serger Settings

For seaming the bag, adjust for a very wide, medium-length, and balanced 3- or 3/4-thread stitch. Use all-purpose or serger thread in the needle(s) and loopers. For the decorative-finish serger settings, refer to Step 1.

Cutting Directions

Cut one 12" by 8" rectangle of quilted fabric. (Fig. 1-3)

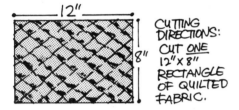

CUTTING DIRECTIONS: CUT <u>ONE</u> 12"x 8" RECTANGLE OF QUILTED FABRIC.

Fig. 1-3

How-Tos

1. **For the reversible edge binding at the upper edge,** use decorative thread in the upper looper and all-purpose or serger thread in the needle and lower looper. Adjust the serger for a narrow and short (2mm) 3-thread stitch. Loosen the upper looper and tighten the lower looper so the decorative thread wraps the cut edge (Fig. 1-4). If

REVERSIBLE EDGE BINDING: LOOSEN UPPER LOOPER

TIGHTEN LOWER LOOPER

Fig. 1-4

the upper thread does not cover the edge entirely, narrow the stitch width or remove it from one of the thread guides or the tension disk. **Serge-finish the upper edge using this reversible edge binding technique.**

2. **To make the serger braid for tying the bag,** adjust the tensions for a rolled edge with decorative thread in the upper looper. Cut two 30" strands of the heavy thread. Insert both strands under the back of and over the front of

the presser foot, to the right of the needle and to the left of the knife (Fig. 1-5). Serge over the strands of thread

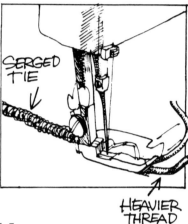

Fig. 1-5

to form the braid. Cut the braid to a 24" length and knot the ends.

3. Find the midpoint of the braid and place it 2-1/2" from the upper edge of an 8" end on the right side of the fabric.

Fold the bag right sides together and serge the lower edge and side, catching the braid in the serging (Fig. 1-6).

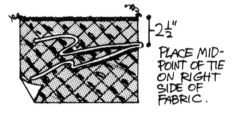

Fig. 1-6

4. Secure the ties and the seam at the upper edge by straight-stitching with a short stitch over the seam where the braid is attached.

5. **Turn right side out,** insert the package of tea, and tie the bag closed with the attached braid.

Ultrasuede Wine Bag

With Corded Design

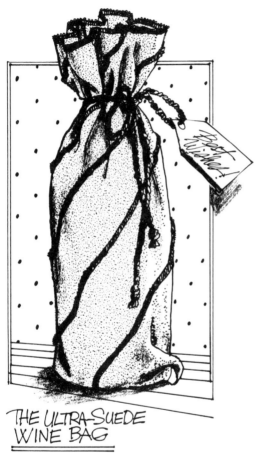

THE ULTRA-SUEDE
WINE BAG

Fig. 1-7

Materials Needed
- **Fabric:** One 14" by 14" square of Ultrasuede®.

- **Heavy thread:** One cone or ball of crochet thread or pearl cotton.

Serger Settings
For seaming the bag, adjust to a wide, medium-length, and balanced 3- or 3/4-thread stitch. Use all-purpose or serger thread in the needle(s) and loopers. For the decorative-finish serger settings, refer to Step 2.

How-Tos
1. **Mark diagonal lines on the right side of the Ultrasuede square 2" apart** (Fig. 1-8).

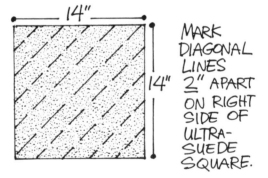

MARK DIAGONAL LINES 2" APART ON RIGHT SIDE OF ULTRA-SUEDE SQUARE.

Fig. 1-8

2. **To make the corded design,** use the decorative thread in the upper looper and all-purpose or serger thread in the needle and lower looper. Adjust the serger for a narrow stitch width and a short- to medium-stitch length (2.5 to 3mm).

Adjust for 3-thread flatlocking by tightening the lower looper tension and loosening the needle tension. Then tighten the needle tension slightly for a corded effect. Fold the fabric on the marked lines, wrong sides together. **Serge over the fold, allowing the stitches to hang over the edge slightly** (Fig. 1-9). Pull the fold flat. Repeat the stitching for each marked line.

FOR NARROW
3-THREAD FLATLOCK:
TIGHTEN LOWER LOOPER
TENSION & LOOSEN
NEEDLE TENSION.

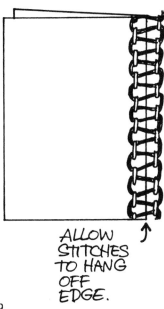

ALLOW
STITCHES
TO HANG
OFF
EDGE.

Fig. 1-9

3. Using the same stitch width and length as Step 2 and changing to a balanced stitch, **serge-finish the upper edge of the square.**

4. To make the cording for the tie, **cut four 60" strands of heavy thread and knot through a hole in the bobbin,** as shown (Fig. 1-10a). (If your bobbin doesn't have holes, ask your dealer if one is available that will fit for winding purposes only.) **Wind until the**

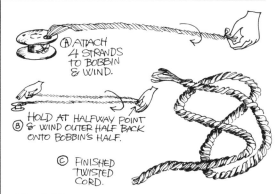

(A) ATTACH 4 STRANDS TO BOBBIN & WIND.

(B) HOLD AT HALFWAY POINT & WIND OUTER HALF BACK ONTO BOBBIN'S HALF.

(C) FINISHED TWISTED CORD.

Fig. 1-10

strands are firmly twisted. Before removing from the bobbin, **hold the twisted strands at the halfway point** (Fig. 1-10b). The four-strand cording will automatically twist back on itself, forming an eight-strand cording (about 30" long) (Fig. 1-10c). Adjust by pulling the cording until the twisting is uniform. **Knot the ends to secure.**

5. Find the midpoint of the cording and place on one side edge of the right side of the fabric, 3" from the upper edge. **Fold the bag right sides together and serge the lower edge and side,** catching the cording in the serging (similar to Figure 1-6 in the Quilted Tea Bag project—Step 3). Secure the seam at the upper edge by straight stitching with a short stitch over the seam where the braid is attached.

6. With a short stitch length, **straight-stitch over the seam where the cord is attached** to secure the ties.

7. **Turn right side out,** insert the bottle of wine, and tie the bag closed with the attached cording.

Potpourri Bag
With Serger-Lace Trim

THE POTPOURRI BAG

Fig. 1-11

Materials Needed

- **Fabric:** 1/6 yard of 45"-wide chiffon or satin (for five bags).

- **Ribbon:** 1 yard of 1/8"-wide satin ribbon.

- **Potpourri:** 1 ounce potpourri.

Serger Settings

For the serged lace, use widest-width, medium-length, and balanced 3-thread stitch. Use all-purpose or serger thread in needle and loopers. For seaming, use a rolled edge and a satin (short) stitch length.

Cutting Directions

Cut an 8" by 5" rectangle from the fabric. (Fig. 1-12)

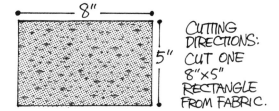

CUTTING DIRECTIONS: CUT ONE 8"×5" RECTANGLE FROM FABRIC.

Fig. 1-12

How-Tos

1. For the serger lace-edge trim, **serge-finish one long edge of the fabric rectangle. Overlap the next row, positioning the needle inside the loops of the previous row.** Leave a 6" tail at the

beginning and end of the rows. For a wider trim, continue adding rows (Fig. 1-13).

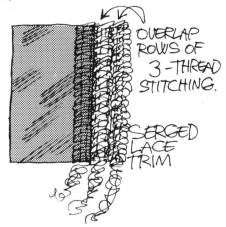

OVERLAP ROWS OF 3-THREAD STITCHING.

SERGED LACE TRIM

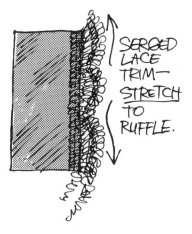

SERGED LACE TRIM— STRETCH TO RUFFLE.

Fig. 1-13

Ruffle the trim after serging by carefully stretching it parallel to the edge.

2. Find the midpoint of the ribbon and place it 1" down from the first serger lace edge you made, on the side edge of the right side of the fabric. **Fold the bag right sides together and serge the lower edge and side with a rolled-edge seam.** Reinforce the lace seam with seam sealant.

3. **Fill with potpourri and tie the bag closed** with the ribbon ties.

Welcome Wreath

This housewarming gift will be a keepsake for years to come, remembering guests from the housewarming party. Or use it for a wall hanging in your own new home. Guests, sign in please!

Materials Needed

• **Wreath Fabric:** 1/2 yard of 45"-wide solid-colored lightweight fabric (test for writing).

• **Bow fabric:** 1/6 yard of 45"-wide lightweight fabric.

• **Fiberfill:** About 8 ounces.

• **Lace trim:** 1-1/3 yards of 1" to 1-1/2" gathered lace.

• **Ribbon:** 1-1/2 yards of 1/4"-wide satin ribbon.

• **Buttons:** Three small heart-shaped or other decorative buttons.

• **Pen:** One permanent marking pen.

• *Optional:* Fabric or stencil paint; screwdriver or wooden spoon to aid in stuffing.

Serger Settings

Adjust for a narrow, medium-length rolled edge. When serging lace on the outer edge, adjust for a narrow, medium-length, and balanced stitch. Use all-purpose or serger thread in the needle and loopers.

Cutting Directions

Cut two 15" circles from wreath fabric. Then cut a 4" circle from the center of both circles. (Fig. 1-15)

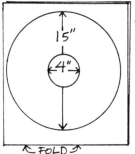

CUTTING DIRECTIONS: FOLD FABRIC IN HALF. CUT 2 15" CIRCLES. CUT OUT THE 2 4" CIRCLES FROM CENTERS.

Fig. 1-15

How-Tos

1. On the right side of one circle, stencil or applique "Welcome" at the top (Fig. 1-16).

PAINT, STENCIL OR APPLIQUE "WELCOME" TO RIGHT SIDE OF ONE CIRCLE.

Fig. 1-16

2. **Place the circles wrong sides together and serge-finish the inner-circle edges.** To manipulate the fabric under the serger, fold the circles in half, as shown (Fig. 1-17).

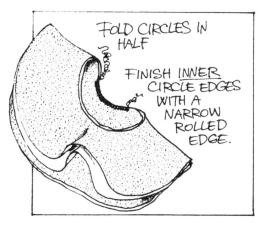

FOLD CIRCLES IN HALF

FINISH INNER CIRCLE EDGES WITH A NARROW ROLLED EDGE.

Fig. 1-17

Start serging, gently pulling the edge under the needle but not stretching the fabric. Continue to refold the inner circle to serge the edge. Overlap the stitches slightly and chain off.

3. With wrong sides of circles together, place the right side of the lace face down on the lower edge of the wreath. **Taper the end of the lace and begin serging,** as shown (Fig. 1-18).

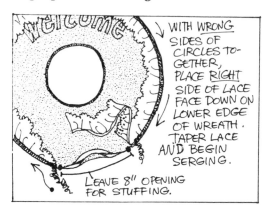

WITH WRONG SIDES OF CIRCLES TO-GETHER, PLACE RIGHT SIDE OF LACE FACE DOWN ON LOWER EDGE OF WREATH. TAPER LACE AND BEGIN SERGING.

LEAVE 8" OPENING FOR STUFFING.

Fig. 1-18

Serge the lace to the wreath with a narrow balanced stitch leaving an 8" opening for stuffing. Do not cut the lace.

4. **Stuff the wreath** with fiberfill, using a screwdriver or wooden spoon, and **serge the opening closed**, overlapping the lace ends and tapering off, as shown (Fig. 1-19).

AFTER STUFFING, SERGE OPENING CLOSED, OVER-LAPPING LACE & TAPERING OFF.

Fig. 1-19

5. For the bow, fold the fabric in half lengthwise with wrong sides together. **Serge the edges** together with a rolled edge, finishing the bow diagonally at each end (Fig. 1-20).

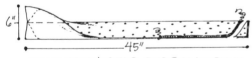

6"

45"

WRONG SIDES TOGETHER, FOLD BOW FABRIC IN HALF LENGTHWISE, SERGE EDGES TOGETHER, FINISHING DIAGONALLY AT BOTH ENDS.

Fig. 1-20

6. Cut off 6" of satin ribbon, fold it in half, and knot the ends. Hand-tack it onto the back of the shirred wreath and use it to hang the wreath, as shown in Figure 1-28 for the Victorian Wreath Project.

7. **Cut the satin ribbon** in two equal pieces. **Fold the bow and tie both pieces of ribbon around the center of the bow** to secure (Fig. 1-21).

CUT RIBBON IN HALF & KNOT AROUND CENTER OF BOW, TYING MARKER PEN & BUTTONS AT ENDS.

Fig. 1-21

8. **Tie the decorative buttons and the pen to the ends of the ribbons.**

9. **Attach the bow** to the lower edge of the wreath by hand-tacking.

Shirred Victorian Wreath

This fabric-decorated wire shape is ruffle-trimmed and is easy to make. It can be simple or extravagant, depending on the fabric and laces used.

Fig. 1-22

NOTE:
WIDE LACE, NARROW LACE, FABRIC STRIP & CONTRAST CASING FABRIC SHOULD BE 2½ TIMES CIRCUMFERENCE OF WIRE FRAME.

Materials Needed

Determine the length and width of fabric required: Measure the circumference of the wire shape (Fig. 1-23).

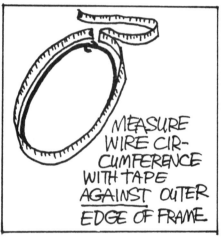

MEASURE WIRE CIRCUMFERENCE WITH TAPE AGAINST OUTER EDGE OF FRAME

Fig. 1-23

For medium-weight fabric, cut the fabric twice as long as the circumference. Cut longer for lighter-weight fabrics.

For a 30" oval wreath:

• **Wide lace:** 2-1/2 yards of 2-1/2"- to 3-1/2"-wide flat scalloped lace.

• **Fabric:** 1/4 yard of 45"-wide taffeta or satin.

• **Contrasting fabric:** 1/8 yard of 45"-wide taffeta or satin.

• **Narrow lace:** 2-1/2 yards of 1-1/2" to 2"-wide flat lace.

• **Ribbon:** 3 yards of 1/4"-wide satin ribbon and 3-1/4 yards of contrasting color of 1/4"-wide satin ribbon.

• **Wire shape:** One 30" oval shape.

- **Rayon thread:** One spool to match color of contrasting fabric.

- *Optional:* Dried flowers to tie onto finished wreath.

Serger Settings

Use a medium-width, medium-length, and balanced 3-thread stitch. Use all-purpose thread in the needle and loopers. To finish the edge of the casing, adjust your serger for a rolled edge with a medium stitch length (2.5 to 3mm). Use rayon thread in the upper looper and all-purpose or serger thread in the needle and lower looper.

Cutting Directions

From the fabric, cut two 3-1/2" by 45" strips. From the contrasting fabric, cut two 1-1/2" by 45" strips. (Fig. 1-24)

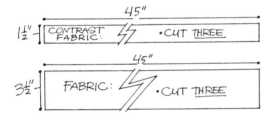

Fig. 1-24

How-Tos

1. **Serge-seam** the two 3-1/2" by 45" fabric pieces, forming one long strip. **Repeat for the contrasting fabric piece.**

2. With wrong sides together, fold the contrasting fabric strip in half lengthwise. Adjust the serger to a rolled hem, with rayon thread in the upper looper, and **serge the folded edge** (Fig. 1-25).

WITH WRONG SIDES TOGETHER, FOLD CONTRAST FABRIC IN HALF LENGTHWISE & ROLL-HEM THE FOLDED EDGE.

•OPTION: USE A CONTRASTING THREAD!

Fig. 1-25

3. With wrong sides together, **fold the 3-1/2"-wide fabric strip in half lengthwise.**

4. To form the ruffles, **match cut edges and layer the fabrics and laces,** as shown (Fig. 1-26).

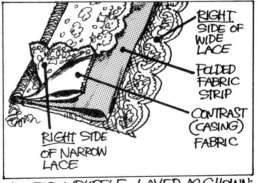

RIGHT SIDE OF WIDE LACE

FOLDED FABRIC STRIP

CONTRAST (CASING) FABRIC

RIGHT SIDE OF NARROW LACE

TO FORM RUFFLE, LAYER AS SHOWN:

Fig. 1-26

Serge together the contrasting fabric casing and the ruffles.

5. **Press the casing layer and the narrow lace away from the ruffle layers** (Fig. 1-27).

PRESS NARROW LACE & CASING AWAY FROM OTHER LAYERS.

Fig. 1-27

6. **Thread the wire through the casing.** Close the wire shape at the closure. **Hand-stitch the ruffle ends together where they meet.**

7. **Cut 9" from the longest ribbon and** **tie into a loop** for hanging. Trim the ends and attach by hand-tacking or gluing to the top back of the wreath (Fig. 1-28).

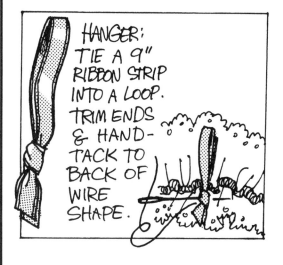

HANGER: TIE A 9" RIBBON STRIP INTO A LOOP. TRIM ENDS & HAND-TACK TO BACK OF WIRE SHAPE.

Fig. 1-28

8. **Cut each ribbon into two pieces.** Tie all four ribbons into a bow and attach to the wire shape by hand-tacking or gluing. *Optional:* Tie dried flowers in with the ribbons.

Firewood Carrier

This nifty carrier totes wood to the fireplace without messing up clean clothes or the carpeting. Carry newspapers in it, too, and you'll save fashions and furnishings from those all-too-familiar black ink smudges.

Wine connoisseurs might also find this multipurpose carrier discreet transportation for two or three vintages.

Fig. 1-29

Materials Needed
- **Fabric:** 1 yard of heavy cotton canvas.

- **Webbing:** 2-2/3 yards of 1"-wide cotton or nylon.

- **Fusible interfacing:** 2 medium-weight nonwoven 3" by 10" strips.

- **Decorative thread:** Cotton crochet thread, buttonhole twist, or other durable, highly twisted, heavy cotton thread.

Serger Settings
When using decorative thread in the upper looper, use a wide, short, and balanced 3-thread stitch with all-purpose or serger thread in the needle and lower looper. When using all-purpose or serger thread in the needle and loopers, use a wide, medium-length, and balanced 3-thread stitch.

Cutting Directions (Fig. 1-30)
Fabric: Cut out the carrier following the layout and measurements.
Fusible interfacing: Cut two 3" by 10" pieces.

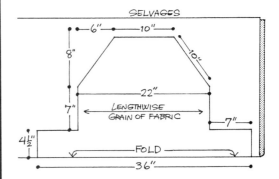

Fig. 1-30

How-Tos

1. **Fuse the interfacing to the wrong side** of the carrier, as shown (Fig. 1-31).

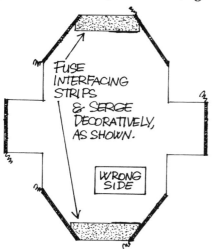

Fig. 1-31

2. **With the wrong side up and decorative thread in the upper looper, serge where shown** (Fig. 1-31).

3. **To self-bind the decoratively serged edges,** fold the serged edge 7/8" to the wrong side. Rethread the upper looper with all-purpose or serger thread and serge along the fold, as shown (Fig. 1-32). Then fold the decoratively serged edge to the right side (encasing the serged seam) and edgestitch.

4. **Hem each interfaced edge** by pressing 1" to the wrong side twice, then topstitch to secure the hem.

5. **Apply the webbing handles.** Fold 1/2" to the wrong side on each end. Position on the carrier, as shown (Fig. 1-33). Butt the folded ends together. Topstitch the webbing in place with two rows of straight stitching. Reinforce the handles at the edges by stitching square boxes, then stitch diagonally.

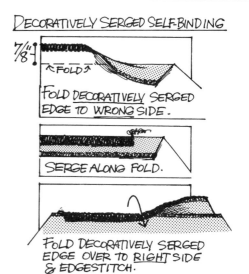

Fig. 1-32

6. Rethread the decorative thread in the upper looper. **Match the unfinished edges, right sides together. Serge a seam.** Press the serged seam toward the diagonal edge and edgestitch through all layers to secure and reinforce (Fig. 1-33). Turn right side out.

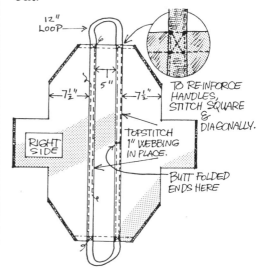

Fig. 1-33

Upholstered Basket

Make any basket pretty and plump with this nifty upholstery technique.

UPHOLSTERED BASKET

Fig. 1-34

Materials Needed

• **Basket:** About 4" diameter wicker, with handle. (Increase or decrease yardages proportionately if you're using a larger or smaller basket.)

• **Fabric:** About 1/2 yard of light- to medium-weight cotton or cotton blend.

• **Polyester batting:** About 1/2 yard of 45"-wide batting (unbonded batting creates a plumper look).

• **Lace trim:** 1-1/3 yard of 1-1/2"-wide trim.

• **Ribbon:** 2 yards of 3/8"-wide satin ribbon (plain or picot edge).

• **Glue:** Thick white craft glue like Slomon's Quik or a hot glue gun.

• **Heavy thread:** About 3 yards (pearl cotton or buttonhole twist) for gathering the serged edge.

• *Optional:* 1 ounce of potpourri for a scented basket. One large ribbon rose.

Serger Settings

Wide, medium-length, and balanced 3-thread stitch. Use all-purpose or serger thread in the needle and loopers. **Optional:** Feed the heavier thread through a cording foot hole or slot, if available.

Cutting Directions

Cut one circle of each, fabric and batting, sized to fit the basket, as shown. (Fig. 1-35)

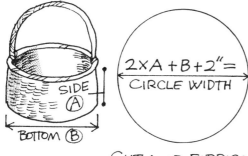

$$2 \times A + B + 2'' = \text{CIRCLE WIDTH}$$

CUT 1 OF FABRIC;
CUT 1 OF BATTING.

Fig. 1-35

How-Tos

1. **Serge the wrong side of the lace to the right side of the fabric circle, stitching over the heavy thread** (Fig. 1-36).

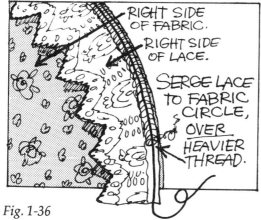

RIGHT SIDE OF FABRIC.

RIGHT SIDE OF LACE.

SERGE LACE TO FABRIC CIRCLE, OVER HEAVIER THREAD.

Fig. 1-36

Lap the lace ends. Do not cut off the heavy thread tails.

2. Trim 1/2" around the entire edge of the batting circle. *Optional:* Sprinkle the potpourri in the center of the batting (in an area no larger than the basket bottom).

3. **Glue the basket bottom to the center of the batting.** Allow to dry.

4. Center the basket and the batting on the wrong side of the fabric circle.

5. **Pull the heavy thread to gather the fabric circle around the sides of the basket.** The fabric edge should fit right under the rim. Before securing the gathering, add scraps of batting to puff out the upholstery. **Adjust the gathers evenly** and tie the thread tails, dotting with a dab of glue and trimming after the glue dries (Fig. 1-37).

BATTING LAYER BETWEEN

PULL HEAVIER THREAD TO GATHER FABRIC CIRCLE AROUND BASKET.

Fig. 1-37

6. **Tie the ribbon around the basket** over the gathering thread with the lace sticking out the top. Tie a ribbon bow between the handles, but tie slightly off-center. Glue or tack a ribbon rose to the center of the bow.

2. *Potluck with Friends*

Adjust-to-Fit Apron

Aprons are underrated. By merely wearing one, you can cuddle a baby without worrying about burp staining your silk blouse or watch fearlessly while greasy gravy dribbles down your protected front. The few seconds it takes to tie on an apron can save extra dry-cleaning bills and washloads. When sewn in fancier fabrics, aprons instantly dress up everyday clothes and add holiday flair.

Adjust-to-fit apron styles make sense because they can accommodate seasonal weight gains and any number of clothing layers. Plus, you can never go wrong giving them as gifts. This one size fits, flatters, and pleases all.

Fig. 2-1

Materials Needed
- **Apron fabric:** 1-1/2 yards of 45"-wide, medium-weight washable cotton or cotton blend. *Optional:* Eyelet border or border print.

- **Thread:** Three cones of all-purpose serger thread to match the fabric. Wind off two bobbins for the top and bobbin of straight stitching.

Serger Settings
Refer to the How-Tos section for serger settings.

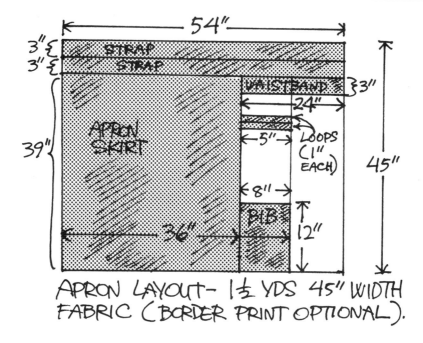

Fig. 2-2

Cutting Directions

Follow the layout as shown for plain or border-print fabric. The finished skirt length, from the waistline, is about 39". If this is too long, shorten as desired. (Fig. 2-2)

How-Tos

1. **Serge-finish one 8" side of the bib** (which will become the top of the bib). Shorten the 3- or 3/4-thread stitch length to prevent raveling. Tension should be balanced. When using a 3-thread stitch, adjust the width to achieve the look and durability you want (the stitch will be exposed on the bib and straps). Use a narrow balanced or rolled stitch to seam and finish the bib and straps. Turn 1/2" of the top of the bib to the wrong side; from the right side, topstitch 3/8" from the fold.

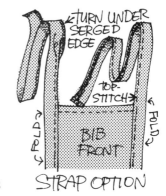

Fig. 2-3 STRAP OPTION

2. **Fold the straps in half** lengthwise, wrong sides together.

3. **Serge the straps to the bib** (using the serger setting in Step 1), right sides together; continue serging to the end of the strap, finishing the raw edges. For a more finished look, curve or angle the strap ends. *Optional:* Turn under the serged seam and topstitch through all layers (Fig. 2-3).

4. **Make the loops.** For easy loop turning, serge a thread chain several inches without any fabric in the serger. Fold the fabric loop right sides together and put the serged chain between the layers near the fold. Serge the raw edges of the loop, being careful not to catch the chain in the serging. Pull the chain to turn the loop (Fig. 2-4). (For ease in turning, cut a small wedge from the fold at the beginning end of the tube.)

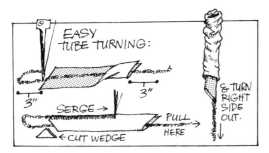

Fig. 2-4

5. With the widest stitch, **serge-gather the upper edge** of the skirt (one of the 36" sides, or the side opposite the border). Gather by tightening the needle tension and lengthening the stitch completely (or, if available, using the differential feed feature set on the 2.0 ratio). If neither of these gathering methods is successful, serge over a heavy cord, secure one end, and pull the cord to gather.

6. Pin-mark the center of the gathered edge of the skirt, the center of the raw edges of the bib, and the center of the waistband. With right sides together, **pin the unfinished edge of the bib to the gathered edge of the skirt,** matching the center markings.

7. **Pin the waistband to the skirt,** right sides together. The bib is now between the skirt and the waistband. Distribute the skirt gathers evenly. With the skirt side on top, serge-seam all the layers together (Fig. 2-5).

Fig. 2-5

8. Open the waistband away from the skirt and bib. **Pin a loop onto each end of the waistband,** as shown (Fig. 2-6). Serge-finish the sides of the skirt

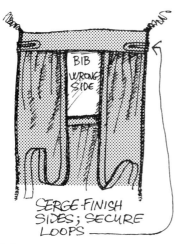

Fig. 2-6

(catching the loops in the stitching). Then serge-finish the bottom of the skirt and the waistband edge.

9. **Press up a 3" skirt hem** to the wrong side. Topstitch from the right side about 2-3/4" from the hem fold.

10. **Fold both sides 1/2" to the wrong side and topstitch 3/8" from the fold** (Fig. 2-7).

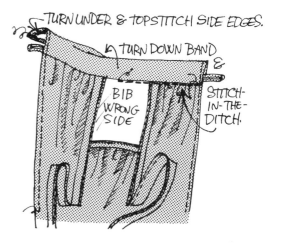

Fig. 2-7

11. **Turn the waistband down** to the finished position (about 1-1/4" wide), enclosing the seam. **Stitch-in-the-ditch to secure the waistband.** At both ends of the waistband, stitch over the previous stitching to enhance durability.

12. **Crisscross the straps and thread through the loops.**

Cinnamon Casserole Mitt

Practical, pretty, and scented with cinnamon, this mitt makes a perfect gift. Folded, it also doubles as a handy trivet. Prefer unscented? Simply leave out the cinnamon sticks or potpourri.

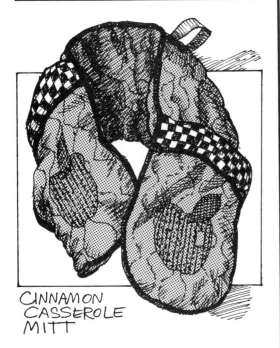

CINNAMON
CASSEROLE
MITT

Fig. 2-8

Materials Needed
- **Pre-quilted fabric** (single-sided): 1/2 yard of 45"-wide fabric.

- **Contrasting fabric** (not quilted): 1/8 yard of 45"-wide fabric.

- **Polyester batting:** 1/4 yard of bonded batting, such as Pellon® Quilt Fleece.

- **Ribbon:** 6" of 1/2"-wide grosgrain ribbon.

- **Essence ingredients:** One package of scented rice, potpourri or cinnamon sticks (about six, three for each side).

- *Optional:* Embellish the mit with purchased or custom-made applique.

Serger Settings
Use a wide, short (satin) stitch that is balanced. Use all-purpose or serger thread in the needle and loopers. *Optional:* Use decorative thread in the loopers.

Cutting Directions (Fig. 2-9)
Pre-quilted fabric: Cut two 27" by 7" pieces for the holder and two 8" by 7" pieces for the mitts.

Contrasting fabric: Cut two 7" by 4" pieces for the trim.

Batting: Cut one 27" by 7" piece for padding.

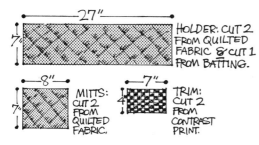

Fig. 2-9

How-Tos

1. **Fold the trim pieces in half, wrong sides together,** so that the 7" raw edges meet. Align the 7" edges of the trim with the 7" wrong side of one mitt. Serge-seam, forming a tube in the trim. Repeat these steps for the other trim and mitt piece (Fig. 2-10).

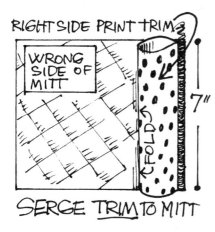

Fig. 2-10

2. Straight-stitch one end of each trim tube closed. Then **insert the cinnamon sticks or other scented filler** and straight-stitch the opposite ends of the tubes closed (Fig. 2-11).

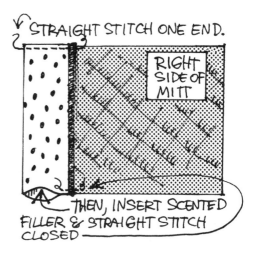

Fig. 2-11

3. **Sandwich the batting between the wrong sides of the holder pieces** (Fig. 2-12). Place the wrong sides of the

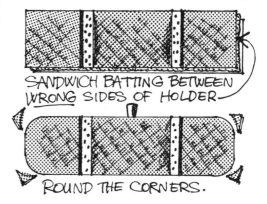

Fig. 2-12

mitts on the right side of one holder piece. Use a coffee mug as a pattern to round the corners uniformly. Pin the ribbon loop to the center of the holder. **Zigzag with a wide, long stitch along the outer edge to compress all the layers.**

4. **Serge-finish the outer edge,** joining the mitts and ribbon in the serging.

Fabric Box with Ruffled Napkins

Your guests will be charmed with this elegant fabric box filled with ruffled luncheon napkins. The napkins and the box are easily made with the serger.

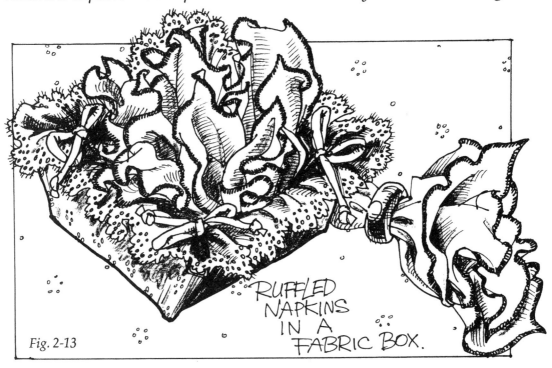

Fig. 2-13

RUFFLED NAPKINS IN A FABRIC BOX.

Materials Needed

- **Fabric:** For six 15" napkins and the ties, use 1-1/2 yards of 45"-wide fabric or 1-1/3 yards of 54"-wide fabric. For eight napkins and the ties, use 2 yards of 45"-wide fabric or 1-1/2 yards of 54"-wide fabric. For the box cover, use 1/3 yard of 45"-wide embroidered or eyelet fabric; for the liner, use 1/2 yard of 45"-wide lightweight fabric.

- **Interfacing:** 1/3 yard of stiff fusible interfacing, such as Style-A-Shade® or Pellon® Decor-Bond.

- **Fusible transfer web:** 1/3 yard of Wonder-Under™ or other fusible web.

- **Eyelet trim:** 1-1/3 yards of 2"- to 2-1/2"-wide ruffled eyelet trim.

- **Rayon thread:** One spool of light-weight rayon thread.

Serger Settings

To finish the napkins, use a rolled edge and satin (short) stitch length with rayon thread in the upper looper and all-purpose or serger thread in the needle and lower looper. (You will need to loosen the upper looper tension when using the rayon thread.) To avoid the "pokies" that may occur when serging on the bias, widen the stitch. Use a rolled edge with a medium (2.5 or 3 mm) stitch length to make the ties. To attach the trim and ties to the box, adjust the serger to a wide, medium-length, and balanced 3- or 3/4-thread stitch. Use all-purpose or serger thread in the needle(s) and loopers.

Cutting Directions

Cut six 15" napkins on the bias, as shown. (Fig. 2-14)

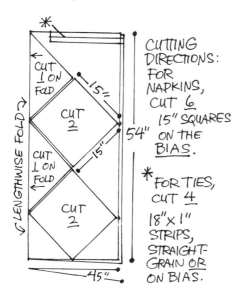

CUTTING DIRECTIONS: FOR NAPKINS, CUT 6 15" SQUARES ON THE BIAS.

*FOR TIES, CUT 4 18"x1" STRIPS, STRAIGHT-GRAIN OR ON BIAS.

Fig. 2-14

For the box, cut four 11" squares, as shown—one of box-cover fabric, one of box-liner fabric (can be the same fabric as box cover), one of interfacing, and one of fusible transfer web. For ties, cut four 18" by 1" strips from the napkin fabric (Fig. 2-15).

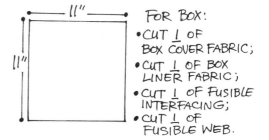

FOR BOX:
•CUT 1 OF BOX COVER FABRIC;
•CUT 1 OF BOX LINER FABRIC;
•CUT 1 OF FUSIBLE INTERFACING;
•CUT 1 OF FUSIBLE WEB.

Fig. 2-15

How-Tos

1. **To ruffle or lettuce leaf the edges of the napkins,** use a rolled edge. Serge a short chain and place the fabric under the presser foot. **Stretch the fabric in front of the needle, holding the fabric taut behind the presser foot** (Fig. 2-16). *Be careful not to bend the needle, which can cause needle breakage and possible stitch finger or looper damage.* The differential feed feature (if your machine has that option) can be used

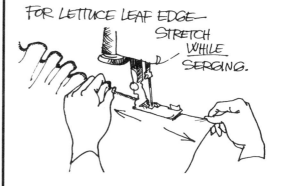

FOR LETTUCE LEAF EDGE STRETCH WHILE SERGING.

Fig. 2-16

to help lettuce-leaf the edge. Set the differential feed on 0.7. Dab the corners of the napkins with seam sealant and trim the thread chains after they have dried.

2. **To make the ties for the box, use the following easy tube-turning method and refer back to Figure 2-3A. Serge a thread chain 24" long** without any fabric in the serger, then **center** the chain on the right side of one of the tie strips. Fold the fabric over the chain right sides together and serge the raw edges of the tie, being careful not to catch the chain in the serging. Gently pull on the chain to turn the tie right side out. (For ease in turning, cut a small wedge from the fold at the beginning end of the tube.) **Repeat for the other three ties.**

3. **Fuse the layers of the box**— cover fabric, fusible transfer web, interfacing, and liner fabric, as shown (Fig. 2-17).

FUSE LAYERS FOR BOX:

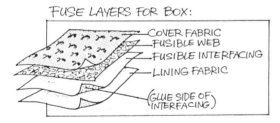

— COVER FABRIC
— FUSIBLE WEB
— FUSIBLE INTERFACING
— LINING FABRIC
(GLUE SIDE OF INTERFACING)

Fig. 2-17

4. On the lining side of the fused square, **place a marking 2-1/2" from each corner. Cut each serged tie in half and glue or baste one tie at each marking,** matching the cut edges. **Round the corners,** as shown (Fig. 2-18).

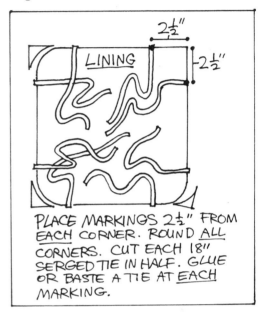

LINING

$2\frac{1}{2}$"

$2\frac{1}{2}$"

PLACE MARKINGS $2\frac{1}{2}$" FROM EACH CORNER. ROUND ALL CORNERS. CUT EACH 18" SERGED TIE IN HALF. GLUE OR BASTE A TIE AT EACH MARKING.

Fig. 2-18

5. **On one end of the eyelet trim, fold 1" to the wrong side.** With the right side of the trim to the right side of the lining, place the folded end of the trim at the middle of one of the sides. **Serge the trim to the box,** catching the ties in the serging and easing the trim around the corners. **Overlap the end of the trim over the 1" fold** and chain off (Fig. 2-19).

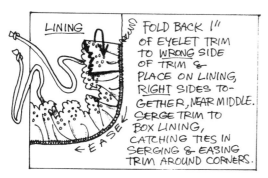

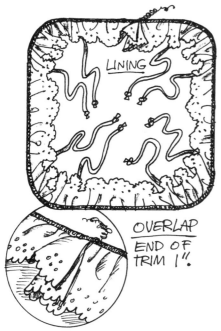

Fig. 2-19

6. Lightly **steam and finger-press the trim away from the box** and then **toward the outside of the box.** The wrong side of the trim will be to the right side of the box.

7. **Finger crease box foldlines 2-1/2" from each edge** (Fig. 2-20).

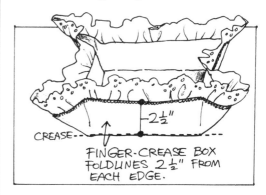

Fig. 2-20

8. **Tie each corner** to form the box. **Knot the end of each tie at the desired length and trim.**

9. Fold the napkins and place them in the box with the ruffled edges showing.

Double Rolled-Edge Placemats

Create one-of-a-kind binding or braid with this double rolled edge, and use it to add an elegant and finished touch to the placemats. The professional look of these placemats disguises their minutes-in-the-making. You will use both the braid and binding techniques.

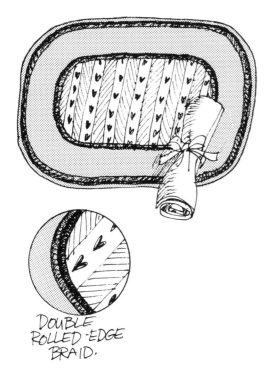

DOUBLE
ROLLED-EDGE
BRAID.

Fig. 2-21

Materials Needed for Six Placemats

• **Fabric:** 2 yards of 45"-wide light- to medium-weight linen or cotton (or blends) and 1/2 yard of 45"-wide contrasting or coordinating print of the same type fabric.

• **Fleece:** 1 yard of lightweight bonded fleece such as Quilt Fleece.

• **Fusible transfer web:** 5-1/2 yards of Wonder-Under or other fusible web.

• **Double rolled-edge braid:** 1-1/4 yards in coordinating colors for each placemat or 7-1/2 yards total for six placemats.

• **Double rolled edge binding:** 1-1/2 yards in coordinating colors for each placemat or 9 yards total for six placemats.

Materials Needed for Double Rolled-Edge Braid

• **Fabric:** 1/2" strips of any lightweight fabric. Use one that blends or coordinates with the upper looper thread colors.

• **Decorative thread:** One spool or cone each of two different thread colors. Woolly stretch nylon is recommended for optimum edge coverage.

Materials Needed For Double Rolled-Edge Binding

• **Fabric:** Long (4" minimum) strips of lightweight fabric that matches or blends with the thread colors. (The width of the fabric strip should be twice the binding width plus 1-1/2".)

• **Decorative thread:** Same two spools as used under Double Rolled-Edge Braid.

Serger Setting

For seaming the binding to the placemats, use a wide, medium-length, and balanced stitch. For braid and binding, use a short (satin), narrow rolled edge.

Braid How-Tos

1. **Serge one edge** of the fabric strip, leaving a thread chain several inches long at both ends of the strip.

2. **Rethread the upper looper** with the other thread color.

3. **Serge the other side of the strip,** holding the thread chain from the first row away from the foot to start the stitching without jamming. Serge, **aligning the needle lines,** as shown (Fig. 2-22). (The foot pressure may need to be lightened. Consult your manual.) The fabric strip should be completely covered by thread.

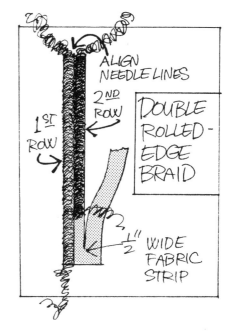

Fig. 2-22

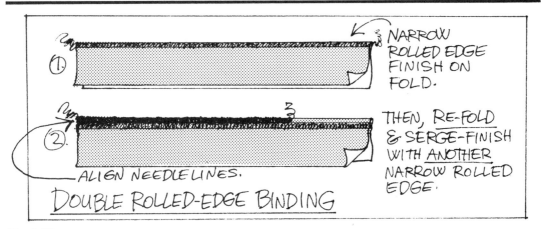

① NARROW ROLLED EDGE FINISH ON FOLD.

② ALIGN NEEDLELINES.

THEN, RE-FOLD & SERGE-FINISH WITH ANOTHER NARROW ROLLED EDGE.

DOUBLE ROLLED-EDGE BINDING

Fig. 2-23

BindingHow-Tos

1. Fold the binding strip in half lengthwise, wrong sides together. **Serge the fold with a narrow rolled edge** (Fig. 2-23).

2. **Re-thread the upper looper** with the other thread color.

3. **Refold the binding next to the previous stitching and serge-finish with another rolled edge,** aligning the needlelines.

Placemat Cutting Directions

Cut out the fabric, fleece, and fusible transfer web, as shown. (Fig. 2-24)

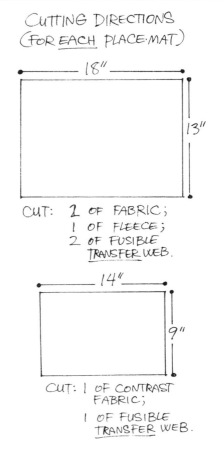

CUTTING DIRECTIONS (FOR EACH PLACE-MAT)

18"

13"

CUT: 2 OF FABRIC;
1 OF FLEECE;
2 OF FUSIBLE TRANSFER WEB.

14"

9"

CUT: 1 OF CONTRAST FABRIC;
1 OF FUSIBLE TRANSFER WEB.

Fig. 2-24

Placemat How-Tos

1. **Fuse the placemat layers,** sandwiching the fleece between the two 13" by 18" fabric layers.

2. **Round the corners** of the placemats with a salad plate and the contrasting layers with a saucer, as shown (Fig. 2-25).

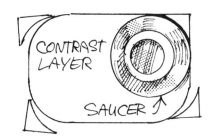

ROUND CORNERS

Fig. 2-25

✎ **Note:** Repeat all the following steps for each of the six placemats.

3. **Center the contrasting layers** with the wrong side to the right side of the placemat (Fig. 2-26).

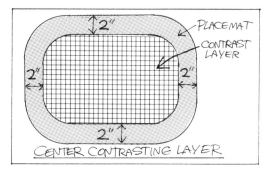

Fig. 2-26

4. **Glue-baste or pin the braid over the raw edge of the contrasting layer** of fabric. (Follow *Braid How-Tos* to make braid.) Fold the braid ends under to hide the raw edges and butt the folds together. **Straight-stitch the braid over the raw edge of the contrasting fabric, in the center of the braid, and through all the layers** (Fig. 2-27).

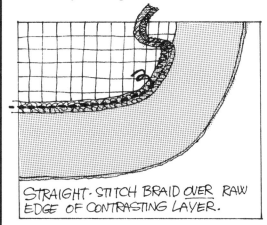

Fig. 2-27

5. **Serge-seam the binding strip to the underside of the placemat,** as shown in Figure 2-28. (Follow *Binding How-*

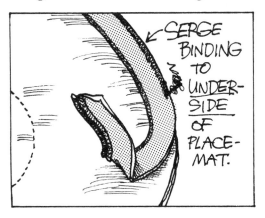

Fig. 2-28

Tos to make binding.) Serge through all layers, easing the binding around the curves and tapering the ends, as shown (Fig. 2-29).

Fig. 2-29

6. **Press the double rolled edge to the topside** and straight stitch between the rolled-edge rows to secure (Fig. 2-30).

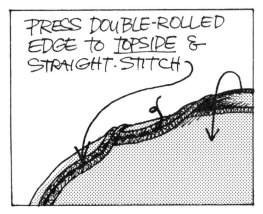

Fig. 2-30

3. *Picnic in the Park*

Instant Picnic Pickup

Spread this bag out and it's a generous picnic tablecloth. When you're finished, simply pull the drawstrings and you have a soft storage bag for toting picnic goods.

Fig. 3-1

Materials Needed
- **Fabric:** 1-1/3 yards of 54"- to 60"-wide, tightly woven fabric like canvas or sailcloth.

- **Cording:** 6 yards of nylon or other durable cording.

- **Grommets:** 16 heavy-duty 1/2" grommets.

- *Optional:* Stain repellent, such as Scotchguard®.

Serger Settings
Use a wide, medium-length, and balanced 3- or 3/4-thread stitch with all-purpose or serger thread in the needle(s) and loopers.

Cutting Directions

Fold the fabric in half lengthwise and find the center of the fabric on the fold. To "round" it into a circle, fasten the end of a string or cord to this center marking (using a push-pin or tack). Pivot and mark the largest possible half-circle. Cut on this line. (Fig. 3-2)

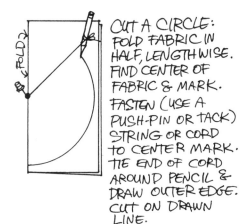

CUT A CIRCLE:
FOLD FABRIC IN HALF, LENGTHWISE. FIND CENTER OF FABRIC & MARK. FASTEN (USE A PUSH-PIN OR TACK) STRING OR CORD TO CENTER MARK. TIE END OF CORD AROUND PENCIL & DRAW OUTER EDGE. CUT ON DRAWN LINE.

FOLD.

Fig. 3-2

How-Tos

1. **Serge-finish the circle edge,** overlapping the stitching at the beginning and the end of the serging.

2. **Fold the circle in half three times to divide it into eight pie-shaped layers** (Fig. 3-3). Along the edge, put a mark

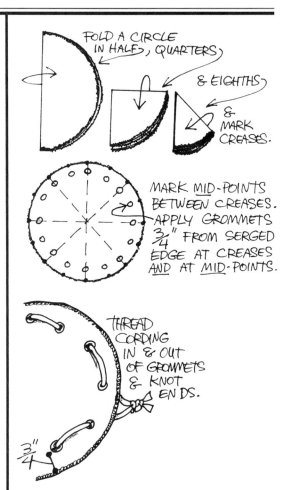

FOLD A CIRCLE IN HALF, QUARTERS, & EIGHTHS & MARK CREASES.

MARK MID-POINTS BETWEEN CREASES. APPLY GROMMETS 3/4" FROM SERGED EDGE AT CREASES AND AT MID-POINTS.

THREAD CORDING IN & OUT OF GROMMETS & KNOT ENDS.

3"/4

Fig. 3-3

at each fold and halfway between the folds, as shown, making a total of 16 marks. At each mark, apply a grommet along the circle edge about 3/4" in from the serged edge.

3. **Thread the cording in and out of the grommets.** Knot the ends to prevent unthreading.

4. *Optional:* **Spray both sides of the finished circle** with a stain repellent.

Roll-up Placemats

These attractive, easy placemats can be made with decorative serging in minutes — just in time for your next picnic.

ROLL-UP PLACEMATS

Fig. 3-4

Materials Needed (for four placemats)

• **Towels for placemats:** Six kitchen towels, approximately 16" by 25".

• **Towels for napkins:** Four fingertip towels.

• **Ribbon:** 3 yards of 5/8"-wide gros-grain ribbon.

• *Optional:* One or two spools of decorative thread like woolly nylon or buttonhole twist for serge-finishing.

Serger Settings

Use a medium- to wide-width, short-length, and balanced 3-thread stitch. Use all-purpose or serger thread in the needle and loopers. Or use decorative thread in the upper and lower loopers.

Cutting Directions

Towels: Cut two of the kitchen towels in half lengthwise.

Ribbon: Cut the ribbon into four 27" strips. (Fig. 3-5)

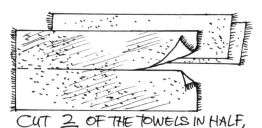

CUT 2 OF THE TOWELS IN HALF, LENGTHWISE.

CUT RIBBON INTO 4 27" STRIPS.

-27-

Fig. 3-5

How-Tos

1. **Serge-finish the long cut edges of the four towel pieces,** using the decorative thread, if desired.

2. Place the wrong side of a half-towel to the right side of one uncut towel, matching the hemmed edges. **Serge the hemmed edges together** (Fig. 3-6).

PLACE WRONG SIDE OF SERGE-FINISHED TOWEL ON TOP OF RIGHT SIDE OF UN-CUT TOWEL. SERGE HEMMED EDGES TOGETHER.

Fig. 3-6

3. **Straight-stitch the ends of the towels together,** and **straight-stitch parallel placement lines for the napkin and utensil pockets,** as shown (Fig. 3-7). The stitching line is 7" from

STRAIGHT-STITCH ENDS OF TOWEL TOGETHER.
STITCH PARALLEL PLACEMENT LINES FOR NAPKIN & UTENSILS, AS SHOWN.

Fig. 3-7

the left side for the napkin and 2" from the napkin line for the fork. Stitch two placement lines 2" and 4" from the right side stitching line for the other utensils.

4. Place the center of one ribbon on the wrong side of the placemat and the upper edge of the napkin placement line (Fig. 3-8). **Straight stitch again through the ribbon over the previous stitching to secure.**

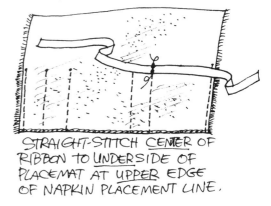

STRAIGHT-STITCH CENTER OF RIBBON TO UNDERSIDE OF PLACEMAT AT UPPER EDGE OF NAPKIN PLACEMENT LINE.

Fig. 3-8

5. Repeat for the other placemats.

6. Place napkins (fingertip towels) and utensils in the pockets, fold the upper part down, and **roll up and tie.**

Chef's Hat

This chef's hat is easily serged and decoratively trimmed with rows of couched serger braid on the band.

Fig. 3-9

Materials Needed

• **Fabric:** 5/8 yard of 45"-wide mediumweight cotton or cotton blend.

• **Interfacing:** 1/4 yard of stiff fusible interfacing.

• **Heavy thread:** One spool, cone, or ball of pearl cotton, crochet thread, or buttonhole twist.

• **Serged braid:** 66" of braid. (Follow the technique in the Quilted Tea Bag project in Chapter 1, page 2.)

Serger Settings

Use a wide, medium-length, and balanced 3- or 3/4-thread stitch. Use all-purpose or serger thread in the needle(s) and the loopers.

Cutting Directions

Cut one 22" circle and one 22" by 8" strip from fabric. Then cut one 22" by 8" strip from interfacing. (Fig. 3-10)

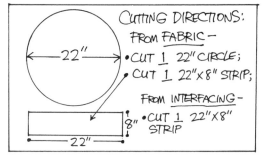

Fig. 3-10

How-Tos

1. **Fuse the interfacing to the wrong side of the 22" by 8" strip.** Fold the interfaced strip in half lengthwise and press (Fig. 3-11a).

Fig. 3-11a

2. Measure down from the fold 1-1/4" and **mark a line parallel to the fold** with an erasable marker. **Mark two more lines 5/8" and 1-1/4" from the first line** (Fig. 3-11b).

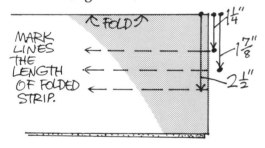

Fig. 3-11b

3. **Place the serged braid on each line.** To form the design, zigzag the braid in place, **sewing through one layer only using matching thread** (Fig. 3-12).

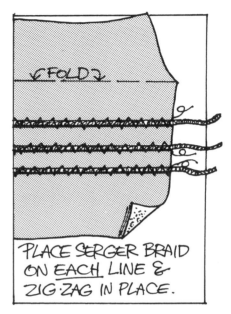

PLACE SERGER BRAID ON EACH LINE & ZIG·ZAG IN PLACE.

Fig. 3-12

4. **Serge-gather the 22" circle.** To gather with the serger, tighten the needle thread tension and lengthen the stitch. (Or, if you have a differential feed, set it on 2.0 for gathering.)

5. Balance the serger tensions. **With the right sides together, serge the short ends of the band.** Fold in half, wrong sides together, along the pressed fold.

6. Adjust the gathers of the circular piece to fit the band. **Serge, right sides together.**

Easy Chef's Apron

This patternless one-yard apron is easy to serge and is one that your favorite chef will enjoy wearing.

Fig. 3-13

Materials Needed

- **Fabric:** 1 yard of medium to heavy-weight cotton or cotton blend.

- **Fabric for casing:** 1-1/3 yards of 1-1/2"-wide bias tape or 48" of 1-1/2"-wide bias fabric.

Serger Settings

Use a narrow, short, and balanced 3-thread stitch, or use a rolled edge with a short stitch length.

Cutting Directions

Follow the measurements in the illustration. (Fig. 3-14)

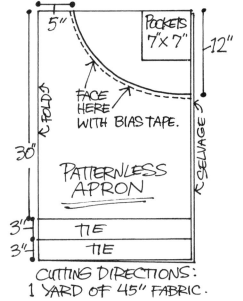

Fig. 3-14

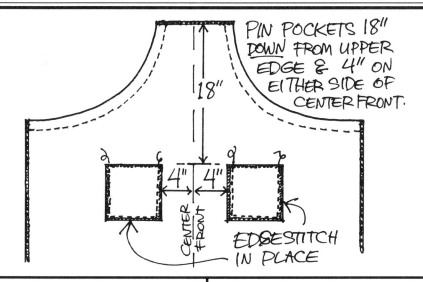

PIN POCKETS 18" DOWN FROM UPPER EDGE & 4" ON EITHER SIDE OF CENTER FRONT.

18"

4" 4"

CENTER FRONT

EDGESTITCH IN PLACE

Fig. 3-15

How-Tos

1. **Piece the two tie pieces into one long tie by serging a short end together.** Press the tie in half lengthwise (to a 1-1/2" width) with the wrong sides together.

2. **Serge-finish the tie, pocket, and apron edges** (except the underarm seam).

3. Face the underarm curves by **serging the bias tape or fabric to the apron** with right sides together. Flip the facing to the wrong side and press. **Straight-stitch along the edge of the bias strip to form the casing.**

4. Pin the pockets 18" down from the upper edge and 4" on either side of the center front of the apron, as shown (Fig. 3-15). **Edgestitch in place next to the serged edges.**

5. **Thread the tie through the casing** and adjust it to fit any size (Fig. 3-16).

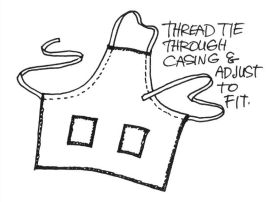

THREAD TIE THROUGH CASING & ADJUST to FIT.

Fig. 3-16

Serged Picnic Set

Before you start packing the charcoal briquettes and chips, serge a picnic table ensemble .

SERGED
PICNIC
SET

Fig. 3-17

Materials Needed
- **Fabric:** 3-5/8 yards of 60"-wide or 5 yards of 45"-wide two-sided quilted cotton or any sturdy fabric.

- **Decorative thread:** One spool of woolly nylon, buttonhole twist, or cro- chet thread to finish the edges of the pockets.

- **Elastic:** 1-1/3 yards of 3/4"-wide elastic.

- *Optional:* 2/3 yard additional fabric and 2/3 yard of bonded polyester fleece for a softer bench cover.

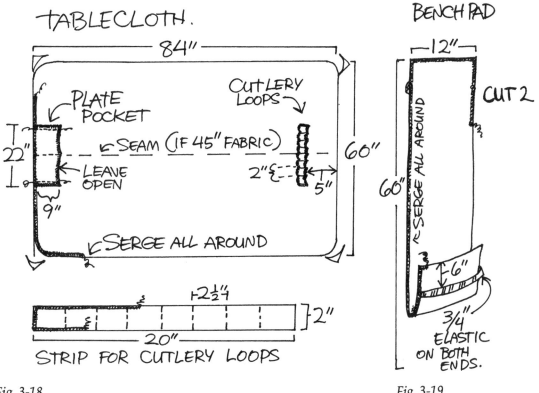

Fig. 3-18

Fig. 3-19

Serger Settings

Use a wide, medium-length, and balanced 3- or 3/4-thread stitch. Use all-purpose or serger thread in the needle(s) and loopers.

Cutting Directions

Cut off a crosswise strip, 9" by the fabric width, for pockets and loops. If you're using 45"-wide fabric, cut the remaining yardage into two equal lengths and serge-seam the two together along the selvage edges. From the serged 45" fabric (keeping the seam centered) or from the 60"-wide fabric, cut a 84" by 60" rectangle. For the bench pads, cut two 12" by 60" rectangles. (Pockets and loops will be cut during construction.) (Fig. 3-18 and 3-19)

How-Tos

1. For easiest serge-finishing, **round the corners of the tablecloth.** Use a coffee mug as a guide for the curve (Fig. 3-18).

2. **Add pockets at one short end** of the tablecloth for holding the paper picnic plates. A 9" by 22" rectangle will hold eight standard 9" plates (four per pocket); adjust the pocket size for smaller or larger plates. With the decorative thread in the upper looper, **serge around the two short sides and one long edge of the pocket. Pin the pocket to the right side of the table-cloth, centered along one short end,** as shown (Fig. 3-18). Straight-stitch where indicated to secure the pockets and form the two compartments.

3. Leaving the serger threaded with the decorative thread, **serge around the outer edge of the tablecloth, finishing the pocket raw edge also.** Lap the ending and the beginning stitches, hiding the thread chain under the serging with a tapestry needle or loop turner.

4. **Add loops to the other end of the tablecloth** to hold the napkins and utensils. A 2" by 20" strip will hold utensils for eight people. **Decoratively serge-finish all sides of the fabric strip. Crease-mark the strip** in half, quarters, and eighths. Markings should be about 2-1/2" apart. **Match the center crease of the strip to the midpoint of the tablecloth,** about 5" in from the finished edge. **Straight-stitch along the crease marks,** approximately 2" apart, until eight loops are formed. The plate pockets and utensil loops also serve as built-in weights, keeping the tablecloth neat, even on gusty days.

5. **Cut the elastic into four 12" strips. Pin the strips on the wrong side of the bench rectangles,** about 6" in from the ends (Fig. 3-19).

6. **Serge around all the sides** to finish the edges and secure the elastic. The elastic loops will slip over the bench ends to hold the pads in place.

7. *Optional:* For softer bench-pad covers, **sandwich a layer of bonded fleece between the wrong sides of two rectangles** for each pad. Compress the three layers along the edge with a wide zigzag stitch, then decoratively serge-finish over the zigzagging (Fig. 3-20).

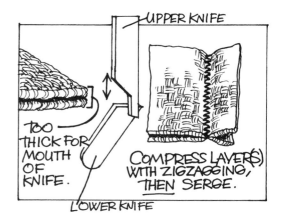

Fig. 3-20

Serged Basket Liners

The perfect touch to a picnic is a serge-lined basket to carry the goodies (Fig. 3-21). Select a basket of any size with a flat bottom and sides that are either straight or curved outward (Fig. 3-22). Before applying the fabric liner, you can dye, brush-paint, spray-paint or stencil the basket.

SERGED PICNIC BASKET LINER!

Fig. 3-21

RECOMMENDED BASKET SHAPES.

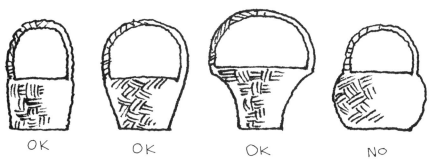

OK   OK   OK   NO

Fig. 3-22

Making a Pattern

Hand-press a sheet of typing or tissue paper into the bottom of the basket and trace the crease that forms where the basket sides begin. Remove the paper, refine the outline, and add 5/8" all around; *this is the basket bottom pattern* (Fig. 3-23).

Measure the distance around the bottom of the pattern and multiply it by three. Measure the basket height—the distance from the bottom of the basket to the upper rim—and add 1". Cut a paper rectangle to these dimensions; *this is the basket side pattern* (Fig. 3-24). Cut another rectangle the same length, but only one-quarter the basket height; *this is the basket ruffle pattern.*

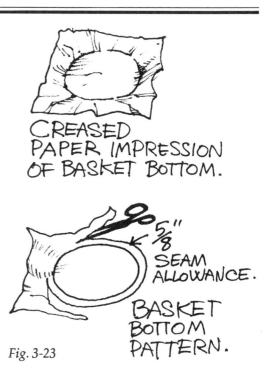

CREASED PAPER IMPRESSION OF BASKET BOTTOM.

5/8" SEAM ALLOWANCE.

BASKET BOTTOM PATTERN.

Fig. 3-23

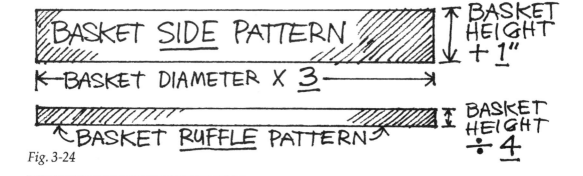

BASKET SIDE PATTERN

BASKET HEIGHT + 1"

←BASKET DIAMETER X 3→

BASKET RUFFLE PATTERN

BASKET HEIGHT ÷ 4

Fig. 3-24

Materials Needed

• **Fabric Type:** Light- to medium-weight woven in solids, checks, or prints. Choose a fabric in which the color on the right and wrong sides doesn't vary much. Avoid eyelets or flocked designs, because textured areas do not respond well to rolled-edge finishing. Consider a contrasting color or a checked fabric as the ruffle (to be cut on the bias).

• **Fabric Yardage:** Determine the yardage required by laying out the patterns on the fabric. Piece the side and ruffle sections if necessary. The layout can be planned on single-thickness fabric because each pattern piece will be cut only once.

- **Cardboard:** The size of the basket bottom.

- **Polyester Batting:** The size of the basket bottom.

- **Heavy thread:** About 3 yards (pearl cotton or buttonhole twist) for gathering the serged edge.

- **Other:** Glue stick or fabric adhesive, washable marker, hot glue gun, or glue.

- *Optional:* Decorative thread for accent, such as woolly nylon, crochet thread, or pearl cotton.

Serger Settings

Refer to the settings in the How-Tos section.

Cutting Directions

Cut one of each pattern piece from the fabric. Also use the basket-bottom pattern, minus the seam allowance, to cut a piece of cardboard and a piece of polyester fleece or batting. Affix the batting to the cardboard with glue stick, No More Pins™ or Pattern-Sta™ spray fabric adhesive. (Fig. 3-23 and Fig. 3-24)

How-Tos

1. **Seam the side section(s) into a continuous circle,** joining short ends, right sides together. Repeat for the ruffle piece(s). Finish one long edge of the side and ruffle pieces with a narrow rolled hem. Use decorative thread as an accent. Reinforce with seam sealant where the rolled edge crosses the seams.

2. **Pin the ruffle, right side up, to the right side of the side section** (Fig. 3-25). The finished edge of the ruffle should be just a bit below the finished edge of the side (1/4" for a small basket, 1/2" to 1" for larger sizes). Fold the side piece down right sides together, folding along the raw edge of the ruffle so it is sandwiched in the fold (Fig. 3-25). Using a 5mm-wide and long 3- or 3/4-thread stitch (and keeping the needle tension loose for ease of gathering), **serge-gather over the fold all the way around the circle.**

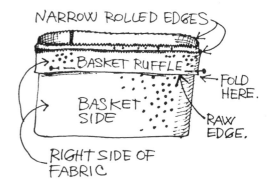

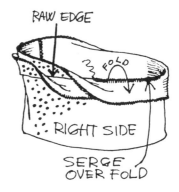

Fig. 3-25

✎ **Note:** Be careful not to cut the starting and ending thread chains; these will be used later for gathering. Press the seam allowance down, away from the rolled edge. If your fabric is soft, spray starch will help maintain ruffle crispness.

3. **Serge a 1/4" row of stitching along the opposite, unfinished edge of the side panel,** as in Figure 3-26. (Remem-

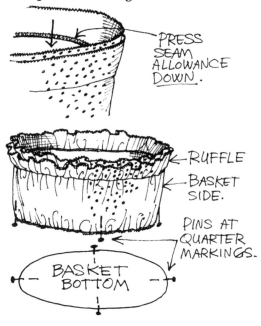

PRESS
SEAM
ALLOWANCE
DOWN.

RUFFLE

BASKET
SIDE.

PINS AT
QUARTER
MARKINGS.

BASKET
BOTTOM

Fig. 3-26

ber to keep the needle tension loose.) Quarter mark the edge with pins or a washable marker. Quarter mark the bottom section as well, as shown. Match the markings on the side and bottom pieces, right sides together. **Pull the needle threads to gather,** adjusting the fullness evenly between the marks. By placing any necessary pins with their points toward (but not over) the cut edge, you can hold the gathers securely while serging over them, without risking damage to your knives.

4. **Serge the gathered side section to the bottom,** inserting a strand of pearl cotton or buttonhole twist under the back of the presser foot and over the front, as shown (Fig. 3-27). The stitches

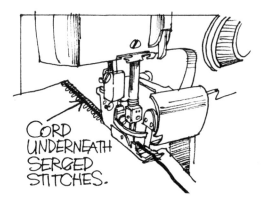

CORD
UNDERNEATH
SERGED
STITCHES.

Fig. 3-27

will form over the extra thread. When the stitching is complete, **use this thread as a drawstring to secure the fabric liner over the cardboard bottom** (similar to applying an ironing-board cover) (Figs. 3-28 and 3-29). Knot the drawstring firmly.

PULL THREAD TO DESIRED LENGTH, GATHERING THE EDGE.

Fig. 3-28

5. Insert the liner into the basket, securing the cardboard base with glue (a hot glue gun works well). **Pull the needle threads from the gathering stitch to form the upper ruffle,** distributing the fullness around the circumference of the basket (Fig. 3-29). Also secure the seam allowance (pressed downward) to the basket with the hot glue gun. Then, arrange the ruffle layers into graceful folds.

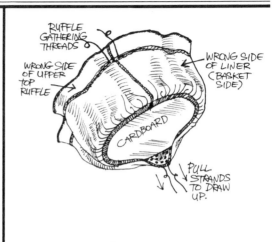

RUFFLE GATHERING THREADS

WRONG SIDE OF UPPER TOP RUFFLE

WRONG SIDE OF LINER (BASKET SIDE)

CARDBOARD

PULL STRANDS TO DRAW UP.

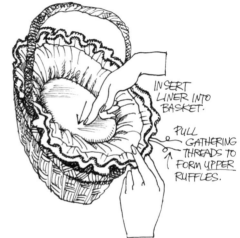

INSERT LINER INTO BASKET.

PULL GATHERING THREADS TO FORM UPPER RUFFLES.

Fig. 3-29

4. *Happy Birthday*

Children's Gifts

Dazzling Dress-ups

There's not a game or toy that captivates kids like costumes. The cape and headpiece can be customized with emblems depicting a favorite superhero or glittering embellishments to dress a king or queen. The clown's costume is a classic for kids of all ages (Fig. 4-1).

DRESS UPS!
CAPE & HEADPIECE / CLOWN'S HAT, RUFF, CUFFS

Fig. 4-1

Headpiece and Cape

Materials Needed
- **Fabric:** 1 yard of sturdy, washable 45"-wide (or wider) fabric (1-1/2 yards for a longer royalty cape).

- **Batting:** 1/4 yard bonded or fusible batting.

- **Ribbon:** 1-1/3 yards of 5/8"-wide ribbon for ties.

- *Optional:* Superhero or star appliques for headpiece and cape and decorative thread for the loopers.

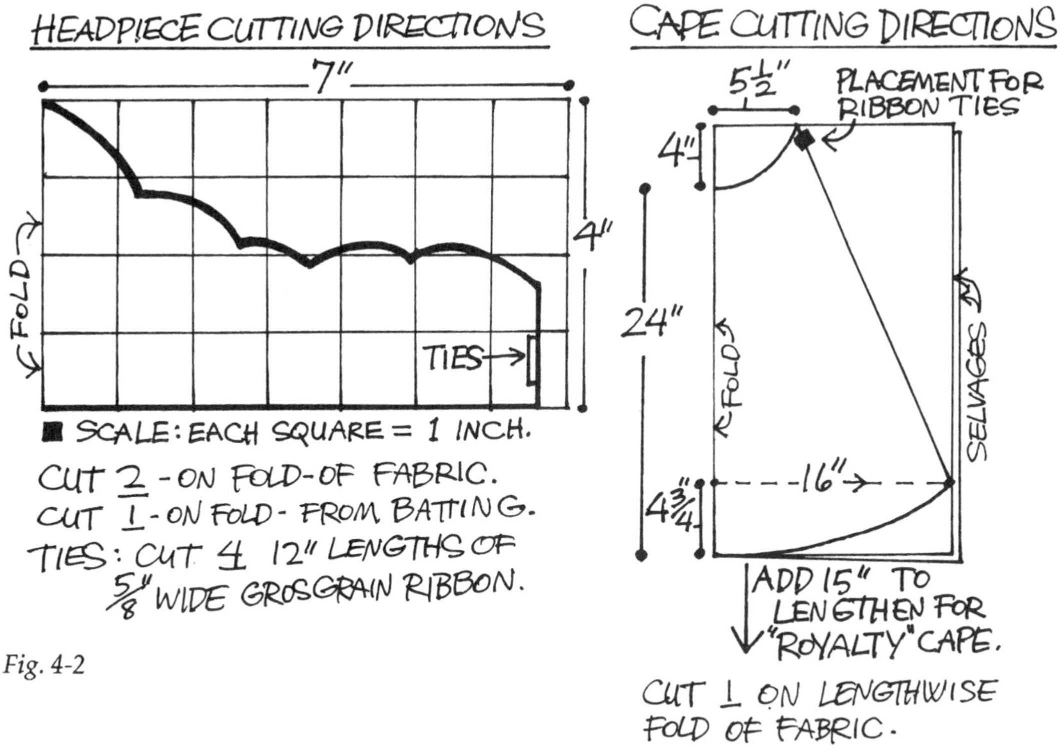

HEADPIECE CUTTING DIRECTIONS

← 7" →

FOLD →

4"

TIES →

■ SCALE: EACH SQUARE = 1 INCH.

CUT 2 - ON FOLD OF FABRIC.
CUT 1 - ON FOLD - FROM BATTING.
TIES: CUT 4 12" LENGTHS OF
5/8" WIDE GROSGRAIN RIBBON.

Fig. 4-2

CAPE CUTTING DIRECTIONS

← 5½" →

PLACEMENT FOR RIBBON TIES →

4"

24"

FOLD →

SELVAGES →

4¾"

← 16" →

↓ ADD 15" TO
LENGTHEN FOR
↓ "ROYALTY" CAPE.

CUT 1 ON LENGTHWISE
FOLD OF FABRIC.

Cutting Directions

Using the grid and measurements, cut one of cape and two headpieces from fabric. Cut one headpiece from batting. (Fig. 4-2)

Serger Settings

Use a medium-width, short (satin) length, and balanced 3-thread stitch. Use all-purpose or serger thread in the needle and loopers. *Optional:* Use a decorative thread in the loopers.

Headpiece How-Tos

1. *Optional:* Appliqué or iron-on a favorite superhero emblem or royalty star on the right side of one piece.

SANDWICH BATTING BETWEEN WRONG SIDES OF FABRIC.

← RIBBON TIES →

Fig. 4-3

2. **Sandwich the batting between the wrong sides of the fabric pieces** (Fig. 4-3). Center two of the 12" ribbon strips on the ends of the headpiece, as shown.

3. **Serge-finish all layers and secure the ribbons.** Reinforce the ribbon ties by folding them toward the serged edge and straight-stitching them (Fig. 4-4).

Fig. 4-4

Cape How-Tos

1. *Optional:* Appliqué or iron on a favorite superhero emblem or royalty star to the right side of the back of the cape.

2. Position two 12" ribbon strips on the upper right side corners of the cape.

3. **Serge to finish the cape edges** and secure the ribbons (Fig. 4-5). Reinforce the ribbon ties as shown for the headpiece (Step 3 above).

Fig. 4-5

Clown Hat, Ruff, and Cuffs

Materials Needed
- **Fabric:** 1-1/2 yards brightly colored poplin or other crisp medium-weight cotton or cotton blend.

- **Fusible interfacing:** 1/2 yard of stiff fusible interfacing, such as Pellon Decor-Bond.

- **Ribbon:** 2-1/4 yards of 1/2"-wide ribbon.

- **Pom-poms:** One jumbo-size pom-pom.

- **Heavy thread:** Pearl cotton, button-hole twist, or other similar thread for gathering.

- **Other:** Hot glue gun or glue.

Serger Settings
Use a medium-width, short (satin) length, and balanced 3-thread stitch. Use all-purpose or serger thread in the needle and loopers.

Cutting Directions
Cut one hat from fabric, as shown. (the finished hat, at the fullest part, should fit the child's head circumference plus 1-1/2".) Also from fabric, cut one 18" by 45" ruff and four 22" by 9" cuffs (for arms and ankles). Cut one hat from fusible interfacing, as shown. (Fig. 4-6)

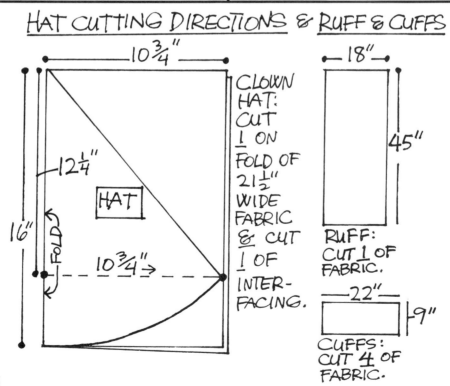

HAT CUTTING DIRECTIONS & RUFF & CUFFS

CLOWN HAT: CUT 1 ON FOLD OF 21½" WIDE FABRIC & CUT 1 OF INTER-FACING.

RUFF: CUT 1 OF FABRIC.

CUFFS: CUT 4 OF FABRIC.

Fig. 4-6

Hat, Ruff and Cuff How-Tos

1. **Fuse interfacing to the wrong side of the hat.**

2. **Position two 12" ribbons on the right side** of the hat, as shown (Fig. 4-7). Serge-finish the lower hat edge, securing the ribbon ties. **Reinforce the ribbon ties** as described and shown for the Headpiece (Step 3, *Headpiece How-Tos, page 52*).

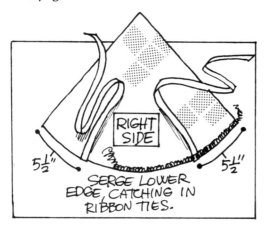

Fig. 4-7

3. Wrong sides together, **serge-seam the hat into a cone shape** (Fig. 4-8). The serging will show on the right side. Glue on a jumbo pom-pom at the point.

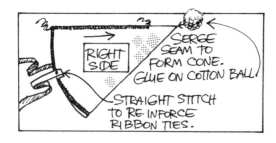

Fig. 4-8

4. For the ruff and cuffs, fold and press the pieces lengthwise accordion-style, as shown, with the right sides out (Fig. 4-9). (Section the ruff into four 4-1/2" sections and each cuff into four 2-1/2" sections.)

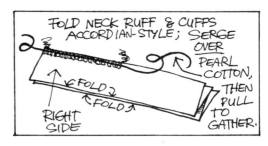

Fig. 4-9

5. **Serge over the heavy thread, catching the two raw edges and the one accordion fold** (Fig. 4-10). Pull to gather the edges: gather the cuffs to 7" and the ruff to 12" (for a 3- to 5-year-old), 13" (for a 6- to 8-year-old) or 14" (for a 9- to 11-year-old). Secure the heavy thread tails by hand-tacking into the fabric and weaving 2" to 3" back through the serging (Fig. 4-10).

Fig. 4-10

6. Position and straight-stitch 12" ribbons on the ends of the ruff and 10" ribbon ties on the cuffs. **Then serge to finish the cuff and ruff ends and secure the ribbons.** Reinforce the ribbon ties as shown for the headpiece in Fig. 4-4.

Card Table Cottage

Embellish a cover for a 34"-square card table to resemble a dream cottage just for kids. The cover is complete with roll-up door, window, and inside storage pockets.

CARD-TABLE COTTAGE-WITH DECALS & APPLIQUÉS.

Fig. 4-11

Materials Needed
• **Fabric:** 4-7/8 yards of 45"-wide reversible quilted fabric.

• **Ribbon:** 1-1/2 yards of 5/8"-wide grosgrain ribbon.

• *Optional:* Iron-on appliques to decorate the house.

Serger Settings

Use a wide, medium-length, and balanced 3- or 3/4-thread stitch. Use all-purpose or serger thread in the needle(s) and loopers.

✎ **Note:** When serging, trim the fabric slightly to be sure you catch the ends of the quilting threads in the serged edge.

Cutting Directions

Cut one 35" square for the roof, two 29" by 35" rectangles for the house sides, two 29" by 40" rectangles for the front and the back of the house, and a 23" by 21" rectangle for the door. Cut two 10" by 8" rectangles for the pockets. (Fig. 4-12)

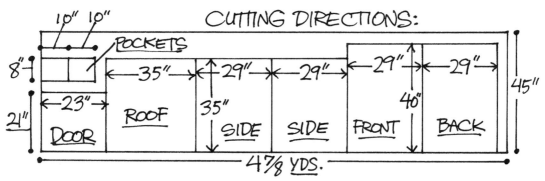

Fig. 4-12

How-Tos

1. For the front of the house, in the middle of one 40" by 29" rectangle, **cut a 14" by 22" door opening,** as shown (Fig. 4-13). Serge-finish the opening. (See *Note* under *Serger Settings* above.)

2. With the fabric reversed, **serge-finish all four sides of the door.**

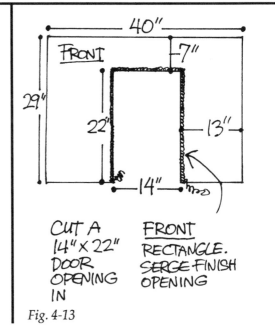

Fig. 4-13

Special gift bags show off decorative serging techniques. We used reversible edge binding on the quilted version, a corded flatlock effect for the Ultrasuede and delicate, serged lace trim on the sheer potpourri bag. See Chapter 1.

This throw becomes a treasured keepsake with crisscrossed serged tucks and a simple serger quilting technique. Chapter 7 tells how.

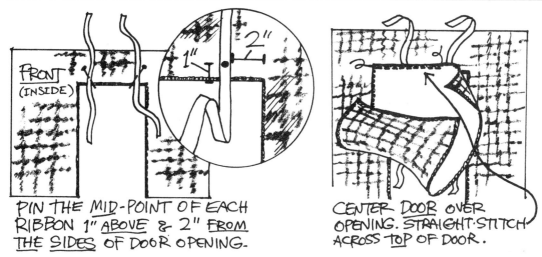

PIN THE MID-POINT OF EACH
RIBBON 1" ABOVE & 2" FROM
THE SIDES OF DOOR OPENING.

CENTER DOOR OVER
OPENING. STRAIGHT-STITCH
ACROSS TOP OF DOOR.

Fig. 4-14a

3. **Cut the ribbon into two 27" strips.**
On the inside of the door opening, **pin
the midpoint of each ribbon 1" above
and 2" from the side edge of the door
opening** (Fig. 4-14a).

4. On the inside, **center the door over
the opening** on top of the ribbon,
matching the lower edges. **Straight
stitch across the top of the door,** catching the ribbon in the stitching
(Fig. 4-14a).

5. In the middle of the 40" by 29" back
piece, **cut a 10" square window.
Serge-finish the window opening**
(Fig. 4-14b). For ease in serging, fold
fabric in half with the wrong sides
together to begin the serging. Overlap
the stitches at the beginning and the
end of the serging.

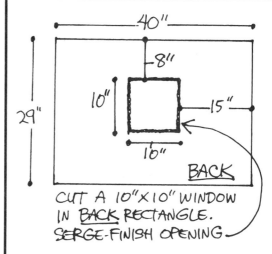

CUT A 10"×10" WINDOW
IN BACK RECTANGLE.
SERGE-FINISH OPENING

Fig. 4-14b

6. **Serge-finish all four edges of the two pocket pieces.** Topstitch three sides of one pocket to the inside of one side piece placing as desired. Topstitch the other pocket to the inside of the opposite side piece.

7. **Serge-finish the sides and lower edges of all four house pieces.**

8. At the top edge, **lap both side pieces 3" over the front and the back pieces,** as shown (Fig. 4-15). Pin to hold in place.

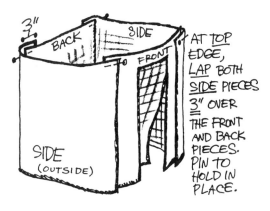

Fig. 4-15

9. With the right sides together, **place one side of the roof piece to the upper edge of one side piece and serge together. Serge the opposite side of the roof to the other side piece** (Fig. 4-16).

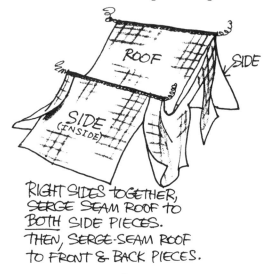

RIGHT SIDES TOGETHER, SERGE SEAM ROOF TO BOTH SIDE PIECES. THEN, SERGE-SEAM ROOF TO FRONT & BACK PIECES.

Fig. 4-16

10. **Serge the other sides of the roof to the top front and the top back of the house.**

11. *Optional:* Iron on appliqué.

12. **Place the house on the card table.** The door may be rolled up on the inside and tied with the ribbon ties.

Panda Sleeping Bag

This sleeping bag is simple to make, and it's also simple to care for — entirely machine washable and dryable. Serge-finishing and seaming stand up beautifully to the usual punishments of tugging, dragging, spills, and frequent laundering.

PANDA
SLEEPING
BAG:

Fig. 4-17

Materials Needed

• **Synthetic fur:** 2 yards of 60"-wide black and 1 yard of 60"-wide white, soft washable pile.

• **Flannel:** 2-1/2 yards of 45"-wide red cotton pile (or 1-1/2 yards of 60"-wide comparable robe fleece).

• **Batting:** A 28" by 42" piece (or about 7/8 yard) of bonded polyester batting, such as Quilt Fleece.

• **Fiberfill:** About 12 ounces of polyester fiberfill.

• **Webbing:** 2 yards of 1"-wide cotton webbing.

• **Velcro®** (or any comparable hook-and-loop tape): 42" (1-1/6 yards) of 3/4"-wide Velcro.

• **Thread:** Three spools or cones of black and three spools or cones of white all-purpose or serger thread.

• **Other:** Chalk or washable marker; spray pattern adhesive.

Serger Settings

Unless indicated otherwise, adjust for a medium- to wide-width, medium-length, and balanced 3- or 3/4-thread stitch. Use all-purpose or serger thread for the needle(s) and loopers.

Cutting Directions

Cut out the fabric, following the directions and grids. (Fig. 4-18 to Fig. 4-30)

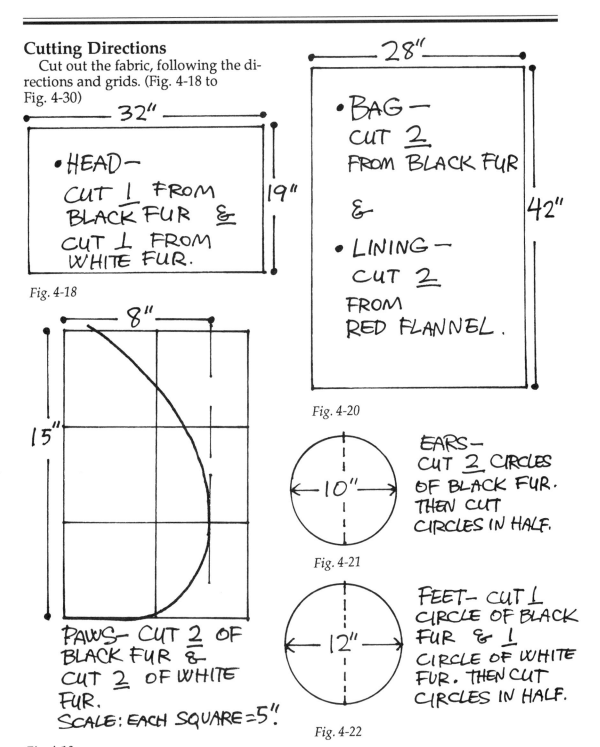

— 32" —

• HEAD—
CUT 1 FROM
BLACK FUR &
CUT 1 FROM
WHITE FUR.

19"

Fig. 4-18

— 8" —

15"

PAWS— CUT 2 OF
BLACK FUR &
CUT 2 OF WHITE
FUR.
SCALE: EACH SQUARE = 5".

Fig. 4-19

— 28" —

• BAG—
CUT 2
FROM BLACK FUR

&

• LINING—
CUT 2
FROM
RED FLANNEL.

42"

Fig. 4-20

← 10" →

EARS—
CUT 2 CIRCLES
OF BLACK FUR.
THEN CUT
CIRCLES IN HALF.

Fig. 4-21

← 12" →

FEET— CUT 1
CIRCLE OF BLACK
FUR & 1
CIRCLE OF WHITE
FUR. THEN CUT
CIRCLES IN HALF.

Fig. 4-22

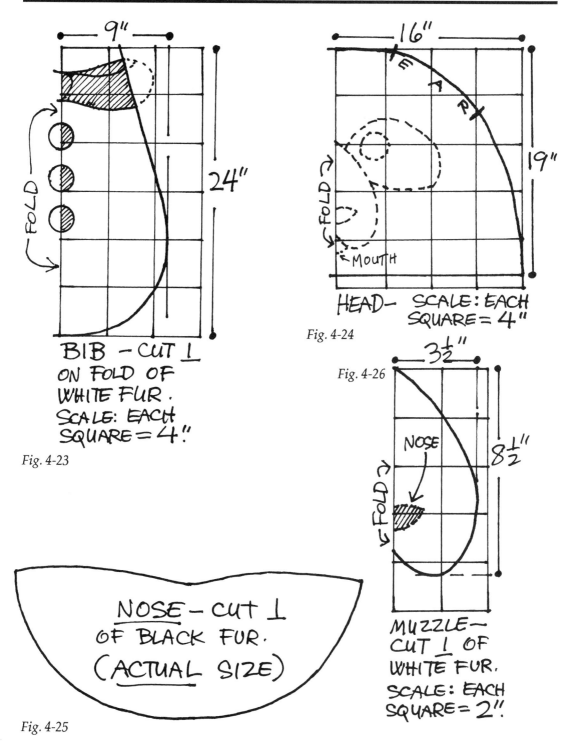

9"

24"

FOLD

BIB – CUT 1
ON FOLD OF
WHITE FUR.
SCALE: EACH
SQUARE = 4"

Fig. 4-23

16"

19"

FOLD

EAR

MOUTH

HEAD – SCALE: EACH
SQUARE = 4"

Fig. 4-24

Fig. 4-26

$3\frac{1}{2}$"

$8\frac{1}{2}$"

FOLD

NOSE

MUZZLE –
CUT 1 OF
WHITE FUR.
SCALE: EACH
SQUARE = 2".

NOSE – CUT 1
OF BLACK FUR.
(ACTUAL SIZE)

Fig. 4-25

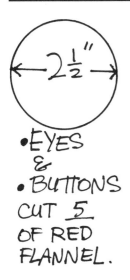

• EYES
&
• BUTTONS
CUT 5
OF RED
FLANNEL.

Fig. 4-27

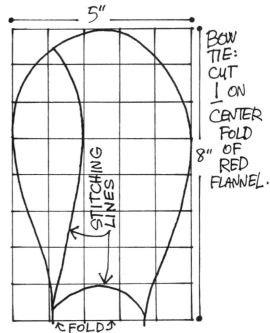

5"

BOW
TIE:
CUT
1 ON
CENTER
FOLD
OF
RED
FLANNEL.

8"

STITCHING LINES

← FOLD →

Fig. 4-29

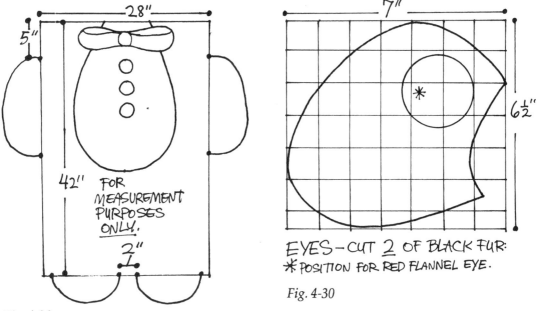

28"

5"

42" FOR
MEASUREMENT
PURPOSES
ONLY.

2"

Fig. 4-28

7"

6½"

*

EYES – CUT 2 OF BLACK FUR:
* POSITION FOR RED FLANNEL EYE.

Fig. 4-30

How-Tos

1. **Fold the 32" by 19" head rectangles and round the corners,** as shown (Fig. 4-24). **Cut the two 10" circles in half** to make the four ear pieces. **Cut the two 12" circles in half** to make the four feet pieces (two white, two black).

2. Use white thread in the needle and loopers. Adjust for a narrow, short, and balanced stitch, and then **serge around the bib.** Thread with black in the needle and loopers (using the same stitch adjustment made in Step 1). Then, **serge-finish the outer edge of the white muzzle,** black fur eyes, and nose.

3. Mark the stitching lines on the bow with chalk or washable marker. Tighten the lower looper to adjust for narrow rolled hemming. **With wrong sides together, fold the fabric on the inside stitching line. With black thread, serge the folded stitching line. Then serge-finish the entire bow.**

4. Using black thread, **serge-finish the five red flannel circles (for the buttons and eyes).**

5. **Topstitch (with matching thread) in the following order.** Use spray pattern adhesive, such as Pattern-Sta or No More Pins to hold the pieces in place before and while stitching. For placement, see the illustration of the finished panda or the cutout grids in Figures 4-23 and 4-24. Vary as desired.

- Wrong side of the **nose to** the right side of the **muzzle.**

- Wrong side of the **muzzle to** the right side of the **white fur head.**

- Wrong side of the red flannel **eyes to** the right side of the **fur eyes.**

- Wrong side of **fur eyes to** the right side of **white fur head.**

- Wrong side of the red flannel **buttons to** the right side of **the bib.**

- Wrong side of the **bib to** the right side of **the body.**

- Wrong side of the **bow to** the right side of **the bib.**

- Adjust for a wide, satin zigzag stitch and sew the mouth. as shown (Fig. 4-24).

6. **Serge-seam the ear, paw, and foot pieces right sides together** (Fig. 4-31). (So that each will be two-tone, seam together a black and white piece for each paw and foot.) Turn each piece right side out. With a balanced stitch, serge-finish the open sides of each piece together.

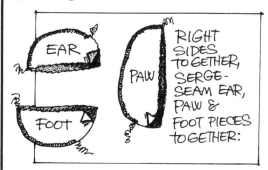

Fig. 4-31

7. **Put the ears on the white fur head,** as shown (Fig. 4-32). **Serge-finish the**

SERGE EARS TO <u>FACE</u>, FINISHING CURVED RAW EDGE AT THE SAME TIME.

Fig. 4-32

curved edge of the head, catching the ears in the stitching. Serge-finish the other (black) head piece.

8. **Straight-stitch the two head pieces together,** as shown (Fig. 4-33). Turn the head right side out and serge the opening closed, leaving a 10" centered opening for stuffing. Stuff the head with fiberfill and serge the opening closed.

RIGHT SIDES TO-GETHER, STRAIGHT-STITCH HEAD PIECES TO GETHER.

Fig. 4-33

9. **Position the head, paws and feet** on the back bag piece, as shown (Fig.4-34); the white side of these pieces will face up with the black side placed against the back of the bag (body). To add fullness, make a 1/2" pleat on each side of the head 3/4" from the side edges (Fig. 4-34). **Serge the head to the back piece as positioned and continue serging around to finish all the edges.**

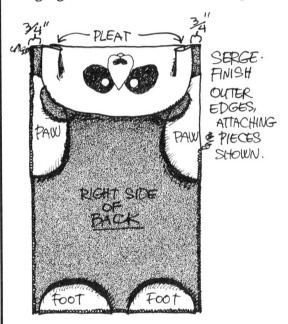

Fig. 4-34

10. Place the right side of the flannel lining to the right side of the back bag with the head sandwiched between; place a batting layer under these layers, to the wrong side of the bag back. With the lining side up, **straight-stitch a 1/2" seam around the left and top sides.** (Be careful not to catch the side of the head in the stitching.)

11. Place the right side of the other piece of lining to the right side of the front bag (body). Lining side up, **straight-stitch a 1/2" seam around the top and right sides**. Turn right side out.

12. **Slip the front lining** (made in Step 11 and turned right side out) **between the back layers** (Fig. 4-35). (The seamed edges will be together.)

13. Matching the unseamed edges, **straight-stitch a 1/2" seam through all four layers across the bottom edge and along the side,** as shown (Fig. 4-35), leaving a 10" opening for turning. Pushing the lining layers out of the way, straight-stitch the remaining unseamed fur layers and batting.

14. **Turn the bag right side out through the opening in the lining.** (The front and back will be seamed together along the bottom and one side; the other side and top are the sleeping bag opening and will be closed with Velcro in Step 15.) Serge the lining opening (through which the bag was turned) closed, wrong sides together.

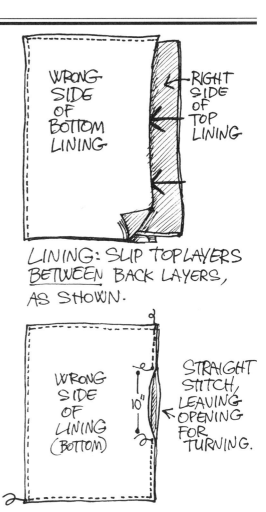

LINING: SLIP TOP LAYERS BETWEEN BACK LAYERS, AS SHOWN.

Fig. 4-35

15. **Straight-stitch** the hooked part of the **Velcro to the front lining at the side opening. Straight-stitch** the looped part of the **Velcro to** the corresponding position on **the back lining.**

16. **To make the ties,** cut the webbing in half (two 36" lengths) and straight-stitch the midpoint of each to the bag on the neckline seam of the bag back (Fig. 4-36). Roll the bag and use webbing ties to secure (Fig. 4-37).

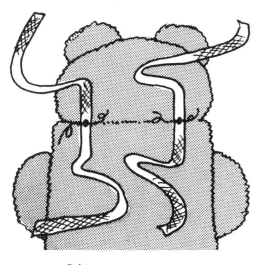

STRAIGHT·STITCH
MID·POINT OF EACH
WEBBING TIE TO
NECKLINE SEAM
OF BAG BACK.

(USING
WHITE
THREAD
ON
BOBBIN.)

Fig. 4-36

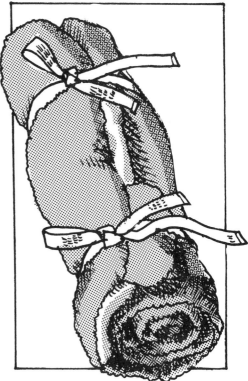

Fig. 4-37

HIBERNATION
PHASE

Gifts for Everybody

Book Cover

Even a simple gift like a paperback gets the "Made-with-Love" treatment when you add an Ultrasuede book cover.

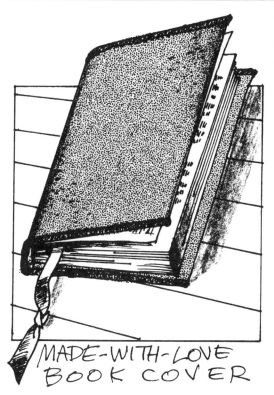

MADE-WITH-LOVE BOOK COVER

Fig. 4-38

Materials Needed
- **Fabric:** 1/4 yard or a 17-1/2" by 7-1/2" rectangle of Ultrasuede or any tightly woven fabric.

- **Ribbon:** 1/4 yard of 1/4" satin ribbon.

- **Decorative thread:** Two spools or cones.

Serger Settings
Use a medium-width, short-length, and balanced 3-thread stitch. Experiment with the stitch width and length to achieve the desired look. Use the decorative thread in the upper and lower loopers and all-purpose or serger thread in the needle.

Cutting Directions
Cut a 17-1/2" by 7-1/2" rectangle. (Fig. 4-39)

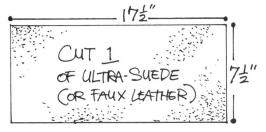

$17\frac{1}{2}"$

CUT 1 OF ULTRA-SUEDE (OR FAUX LEATHER)

$7\frac{1}{2}"$

Fig. 4-39

How-Tos
1. From the right side, serge-finish both short ends.

2. With the wrong sides together, **fold the ends of the rectangle toward the middle,** leaving a 2" space between the edges (Fig. 4-40).

Fig. 4-40

3. Place the ribbon at the midpoint of the top edge for a bookmark. **Serge the upper and lower edges,** then secure the ends by threading the thread chains back through the stitching. *Optional:* Serge around all four edges.

Beach Roll-Up

This nylon tote carries your accessories and wraps around your towel as a carryall for the beach. The five pockets, closed with Velcro, keep the contents dry and sand-free.

Fig. 4-41

Materials Needed

- **Fabric:** 1/3 yard of 45"-wide Gore-Tex®, nylon pack cloth, ripstop, or any tightly woven, water-repellent fabric.

- **Vinyl:** 2/3 yard of lightweight clear 45"-wide vinyl.

- **Velcro** (or any comparable hook-and-loop tape): 32" of 3/4"-wide Velcro.

- **Webbing:** 1-2/3 yard of 1"-wide cotton or nylon.

Serger Settings

Use a medium- to wide-width, medium-length, and balanced 3- or 3/4-thread stitch. A size 11 (#70) needle works best when serging the vinyl. Do not pin, as the pinning will leave holes in the vinyl. Use all-purpose or serger thread in the needle(s) and loopers.

Cutting Directions (Fig. 4-42)

Fabric: Cut one 34" by 10" rectangle.

Vinyl: Cut one 34" by 10" rectangle and one 30" by 10" rectangle.

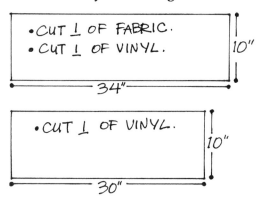

Fig. 4-42

How-Tos

1. Cut one 30" Velcro strip. With the Velcro on top, **serge the hooked strip to one long end of the 30" vinyl rectangle.**

2. Place the 34" by 10" vinyl rectangle on the wrong side of the fabric rectangle. Using a coffee mug as a pattern, **round the corners** uniformly at

the right side (with vinyl side up), as shown (Fig. 4-43). **Serge the looped**

PLACE VINYL ON WRONG SIDE OF FABRIC. ROUND CORNERS ON ONE END. SERGE VELCRO TO TOP EDGE, AS SHOWN.

Fig. 4-43

side of the 30" Velcro strip to the top edge of the two 34" rectangles, beginning at the upper left side.

3. Press the Velcro strips together, matching the cut edges of the vinyl and the fabric rectangles. **Serge the remaining layers together** from one end of the Velcro around to the other end (Fig. 4-44), stitching over the ends of the Velcro to secure.

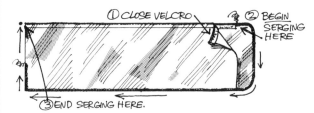

Fig. 4-44

4. On the fabric side, **mark various-size sections,** as shown (Fig. 4-45).

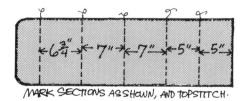

MARK SECTIONS AS SHOWN, AND TOPSTITCH.

Fig. 4-45

(Make certain that the marking on the rounded end will catch the smaller vinyl rectangle and Velcro in the stitching.) With a long stitch length, **topstitch on the markings to form the sections,** sewing through the Velcro strip to secure the stitching at the upper edge.

5. Cut the remaining Velcro into two equal lengths. **Topstitch the hooked strips onto the vinyl side** of the rounded end, 1" from each side edge. **Topstitch the looped strips onto the fabric side over the stitching of the second section,** 1" in from each side edge (Fig. 4-46).

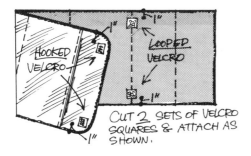

Fig. 4-46

6. Cut the webbing into a 10" and a 50" length. Serge-finish the cut ends. On the fabric side, **topstitch each end of the 10" strip over the second top-stitching line and the ends of the 48" strip to the rounded end** of the roll-up, as shown (Fig. 4-47). The short web-bing can be used as a handle, as shown in Figure 4-41, or as an anchor when the long webbing is used as a shoulder strap.

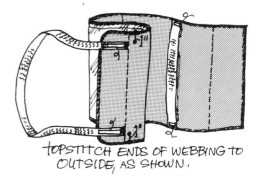

Fig. 4-47

7. **Wrap the tote around a rolled-up beach towel,** insert the long strap under the shorter strap, toss over your shoulder, and head for the beach!

Gifts for Him

Sport Towel

This easy-to-make sport towel is a fast and unique treat for the man on your gift list. Made from terry cloth yardage or a large bath towel, this handy exercise accessory has two large pockets for holding keys, wallet, or watch.

Fig. 4-48

Materials Needed
- **Fabric:** 2/3 yard of 45"-wide terry cloth or one large bath towel, at least 24" by 45".

Serger Settings
Use a wide, short, and balanced 3- or 3/4-thread stitch. Use all-purpose or serger thread of contrasting color in the needle(s) and loopers. *Optional:* Use decorative thread, such as woolly nylon or buttonhole twist, in the upper and lower loopers for a more decorative accent.

Cutting Directions
Cut one 45" by 10" rectangle for the towel and two 9" by 10" rectangles for the pockets. (Fig. 4-49)

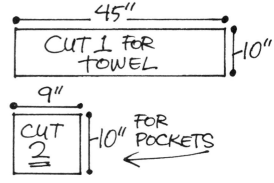

Fig. 4-49

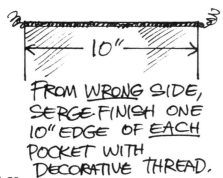

FROM WRONG SIDE, SERGE-FINISH ONE 10" EDGE OF EACH POCKET WITH DECORATIVE THREAD.

Fig. 4-50

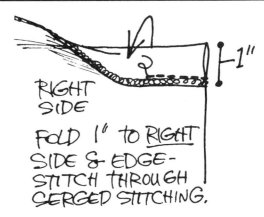

RIGHT SIDE

FOLD 1" TO RIGHT SIDE & EDGE-STITCH THROUGH SERGED STITCHING.

How-Tos

1. On the wrong side, serge-finish one 10" edge of each pocket piece. Fold 1" to the right side and edgestitch through the serged stitching to secure the pocket hem (Fig. 4-50).

2. Place the wrong side of each pocket piece to the right side of the towel at each end, matching the cut edges. Using a coffee mug as a pattern, round the corners uniformly. Serge-finish the outer edge, joining the pockets in the serging (Fig. 4-51).

PLACE WRONG SIDE OF POCKETS ONTO RIGHT SIDE OF TOWEL. ROUND CORNERS. THEN SERGE-FINISH OUTER EDGES WITH DECORATIVE THREAD.

Fig. 4-51

Shoe Wallet

This small wallet is large enough for change, bills and even a credit card. It is an excellent gift for the bicyclist, walker or jogger. Waterproof and lightweight, it fits any lace-up shoe.

HANDY SHOE WALLET!

Fig. 4-52

Materials Needed
- **Fabric:** 1/8 yard of ripstop nylon or other waterproof fabric.

- **Velcro** (or any comparable hook-and-loop tape): 3/4" square.

Serger Settings
Adjust to a narrow rolled-edge stitch or a narrow, short (satin), and balanced 3-thread stitch. Use all-purpose or serger thread in the needle and loopers. *Optional:* Use woolly stretch nylon in the upper looper.

Cutting Directions
Cut two 8" by 3" rectangles for the wallet and one 6" by 2-1/4" rectangle for the strap. (Fig. 4-53)

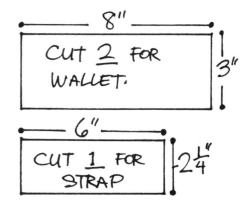

Fig. 4-53

How-Tos
1. **Place the wrong sides of the 8" by 3" rectangles together and serge-finish the four sides.**

2. With the wrong sides together, **fold the strap in half lengthwise and serge-finish** the four sides.

3. **Straight-stitch the hooked 3/4"
square of Velcro to the underside at
one end of the strap. Stitch the looped
square of Velcro to the topside side
of the wallet** close to one end (Fig. 4-
54).

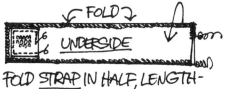

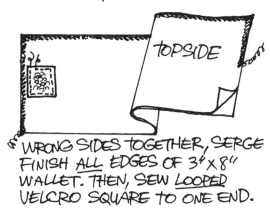

FOLD STRAP IN HALF, LENGTH-
WISE. SERGE·FINISH ALL
SIDES. THEN, SEW HOOKED
VELCRO SQUARE TO ONE END.

WRONG SIDES TOGETHER, SERGE
FINISH ALL EDGES OF 3"X 8"
WALLET. THEN, SEW LOOPED
VELCRO SQUARE TO ONE END.

Fig. 4-54

4. **Topstitch the under side of the
other end of the strap to the top side
of the wallet** 1-1/2" from the Velcro
square, as shown (Fig. 4-55).

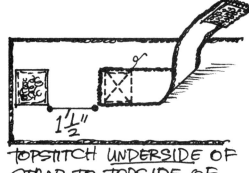

TOPSTITCH UNDERSIDE OF
STRAP TO TOPSIDE OF
WALLET, 1½" FROM VELCRO
SQUARE.

Fig. 4-55

5. **To make the wallet pocket, fold
3-1/2" of the other end of the wallet to
the wrong side and edgestitch close to
the serged edges on both sides to
secure** (Fig. 4-56).

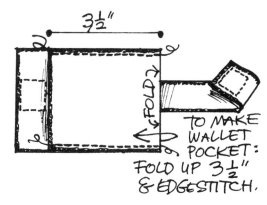

TO MAKE
WALLET
POCKET:
FOLD UP 3½"
& EDGESTITCH.

Fig. 4-56

6. **Insert the strap under the shoelaces
of the shoe and attach to the front of
the wallet.**

Wrist Wallet

Ever wonder where walkers and joggers hide their keys? Questionably safe and admittedly uncomfortable or inconvenient hiding spots prevail. But your favorite athletes will thank you every time they stash keys and money in this nearly weightless wrist wallet.

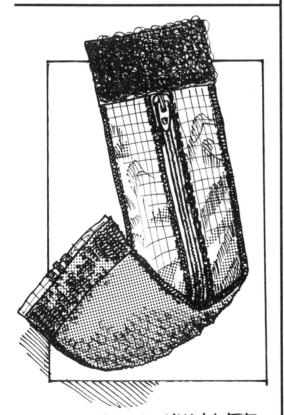

Fig. 4-57   **WRIST WALLET FOR JOGGERS & WALKERS**

Materials Needed

- **Fabric:** 1/8 yard (or scraps) of ripstop nylon or other lightweight waterproof fabric.

- **Liner:** 1/8 yard of terry cloth (or scraps).

- **Zipper:** 12" length lightweight plastic coil teeth.

- **Velcro** (or any comparable hook-and-loop tape): A 3" length of 3/4"-wide and a 3" length of 1-1/2"-wide Velcro.

Serger Settings

Adjust to a narrow rolled edge, short (satin) 3-thread stitch. Use all-purpose or serger thread in the needle and loopers. *Optional:* Use woolly stretch nylon in the upper looper.

Cutting Directions

Cut one 11" by 3-1/2" piece and one 3 1/2" by 2" piece from ripstop nylon. Cut one 11" by 3-1/2" piece from terry cloth. (Fig. 4-58)

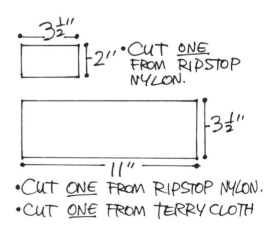

Fig. 4-58

How-Tos

1. **Cut the 11" by 3-1/2" nylon piece into two pieces,** one 11" by 1-1/2" and one 11" by 2". Finish one 11" edge of each strip, right side up, with a rolled edge.

2. **Apply the zipper.** Place the serge-finished edges on the right side of the zipper, next to the teeth. Position the fabric on the zipper as shown, 1/4" above the lower zipper stop (Fig. 4-59). **Edgestitch close to the serging and teeth with a straight stitch.**

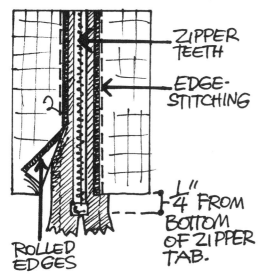

ZIPPER APPLICATION

ZIPPER TEETH

EDGE-STITCHING

1/4" FROM BOTTOM OF ZIPPER TAB.

ROLLED EDGES

Fig. 4-59

3. **Fold the 3-1/2" by 2" nylon piece in half,** lengthwise (to 3-1/2" by 1"). **Serge-finish both** 3-1/2" sides. **Edgestitch the serged strip across the zipper,** 1/2" from the fabric edges, as shown (Fig. 4-60).

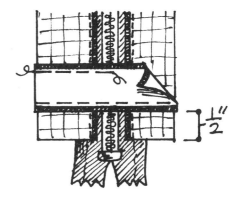

EDGESTITCH SERGED STRIP OVER ZIPPER.

1/2"

Fig. 4-60

4. With the wrong sides of the zippered nylon and terry cloth rectangles together, **serge-seam and finish both 11" edges.**

5. Use the 3" length of the 3/4"-wide Velcro, hooked side only. **Lap the Velcro piece over the wallet end,** as

shown. **Edge-stitch.** Trim off the zipper tape ends (Fig. 4-61).

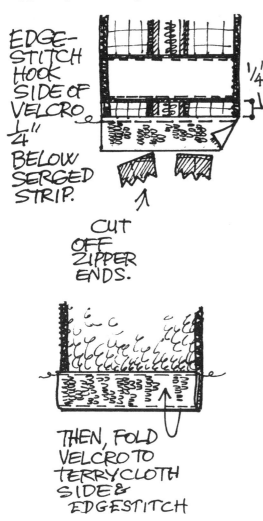

Fig. 4-61

6. **Fold under the stitched-on Velcro strip to the terry cloth side** so it is positioned directly under the serged nylon strip. **Edgestitch from the nylon strip side,** catching the Velcro piece underneath.

7. Unzip the zipper about 2". **Lap the 1-1/2" by 3" piece of Velcro** (looped side) **1/4" over the right side of the terry cloth** on the unfinished end of the wallet. Edgestitch. **Fold this Velcro piece to the zippered right side, encasing the raw edges.** Edgestitch the remaining three sides of the Velcro to secure (Fig. 4-62).

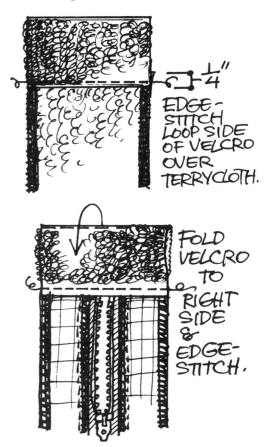

Fig. 4-62

✎ **Note:** The wallet laps around the wrist, zippered side up, with the adjustable Velcro fastener.

Gifts for Her

Handy Tote

This roomy tote can be used for any occasion and makes a perfect gift for that special friend. The professional finished quality gives the look of ready-made travel accessories yet beats the cost of retail prices.

Fig. 4-63

Materials Needed
- **Fabric:** 3/4 yard of synthetic suede or leather.

- **Webbing:** 2 yards of 1"-wide cotton or polyester webbing.

Serger Settings
Use a wide- to medium-width, medium-length, and balanced 3-thread stitch. Use all-purpose or serger thread in the needle and loopers. *Optional:* For serge-finishing the casing and bag edges, use decorative thread in the upper and lower loopers.

Cutting Directions
For the bag, cut one rectangle 34" by 25". For the casing, cut one rectangle 32" by 2-1/2" (or 1" wider than the strap). (Fig. 4-64)

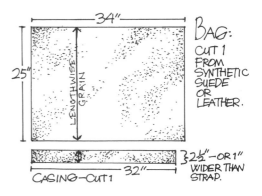

Fig. 4-64

How-Tos
1. **Serge-finish the casing and bag edges. Topstitch the casing to the right side of the bag** 2" from the top

edge and 1" from either end (Fig. 4-65).

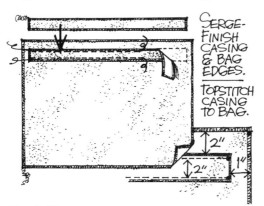

Fig. 4-65

2. Fold the bag right sides together and **straight-stitch the bottom edge** (Fig. 4-66). Turn right side out.

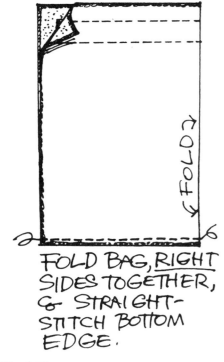

FOLD BAG, RIGHT SIDES TOGETHER, & STRAIGHT-STITCH BOTTOM EDGE.

Fig. 4-66

3. Form a 2"-deep pleat at the bottom. Then, from the **inside of the pleat, straight-stitch through two layers,** as shown, **along the side foldline** to secure the pleat (Fig. 4-67).

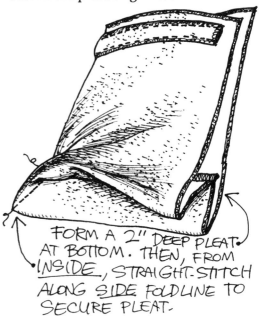

FORM A 2" DEEP PLEAT AT BOTTOM. THEN, FROM INSIDE, STRAIGHT-STITCH ALONG SIDE FOLDLINE TO SECURE PLEAT.

Fig. 4-67

4. **Run the webbing through the casing** (Fig. 4-68). Fold the webbing

RUN WEBBING THROUGH CASING...

Fig. 4-68

back and **straight-stitch the side seam** to 3-1/2" above the bottom (Fig. 4-69).

...FOLD WEBBING BACK & STRAIGHT STITCH SIDE SEAM TO 3½" ABOVE BOTTOM.

Fig. 4-69

5. Stagger both ends of the webbing inside the bottom of the bag, as shown (Fig. 4-70). Double-stitch through all layers to secure the ends. Pull up the webbing to gather the top edges.

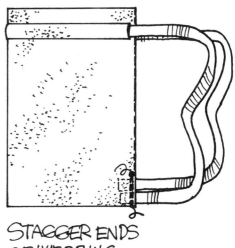

STAGGER ENDS OF WEBBING INSIDE BOTTOM OF BAG. DOUBLE STITCH THROUGH ALL LAYERS TO SECURE ENDS.

Fig. 4-70

Kitty Caddy

This pet is the perfect companion. She dutifully tends handsewing tools, television remote control, viewing guides, and reading glasses — all without the usual feline fur and litter box irritations.

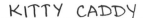

Fig. 4-71

Materials Needed

• **Fabric:** 1 yard of 45"-wide napped fabric such as corduroy, suede or velveteen (for the cat and runner).

• **Velcro** (or any comparable hook-and-loop tape): 7" of 3/4"-wide Velcro.

• **Stuffing:** Approximately 4 ounces of polyester fiberfill.

• **Embroidery floss or fabric paint** (for the face features): The colors of your choice.

• *Optional:* Sew-on eyes.

Serger Settings

Use a medium-width, medium-length, and balanced 3-thread stitch with all-purpose or serger thread in the needle and loopers.

Cutting Directions

Cut one 13-1/2" by 24" runner, one large 7-1/2" by 8" pocket, and one small 4" by 6" pocket (or make it the width of the TV remote control plus 1"). Using the grids and measurements illustrated, cut two cat bodies, two faces, two tails, and one gusset. (Fig. 4-72 to Fig. 4-75)

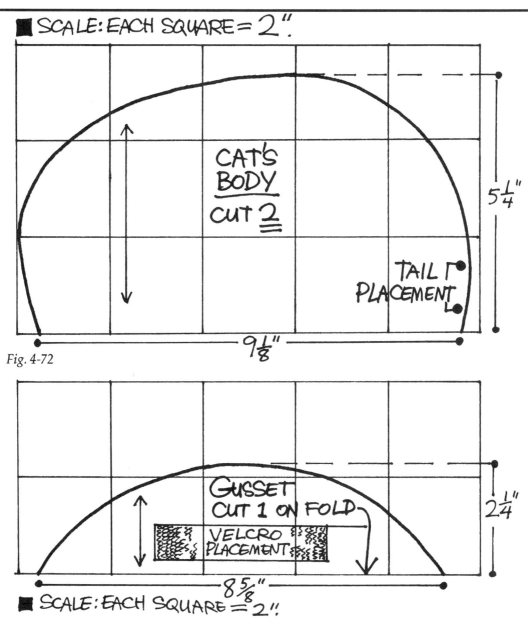

■ SCALE: EACH SQUARE = 2".

CAT'S BODY CUT 2

TAIL PLACEMENT

$5\frac{1}{4}"$

$9\frac{1}{8}"$

Fig. 4-72

GUSSET CUT 1 ON FOLD

VELCRO PLACEMENT

$2\frac{1}{4}"$

$8\frac{5}{8}"$

■ SCALE: EACH SQUARE = 2".

Fig. 4-73

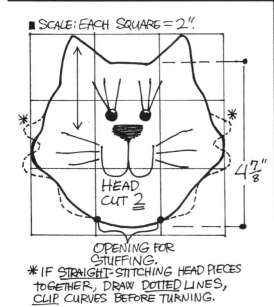

■ SCALE: EACH SQUARE = 2".

HEAD
CUT 2

$4\frac{7}{8}$"

OPENING FOR
STUFFING.
* IF STRAIGHT-STITCHING HEAD PIECES
TOGETHER, DRAW DOTTED LINES,
CLIP CURVES BEFORE TURNING.

Fig. 4-74

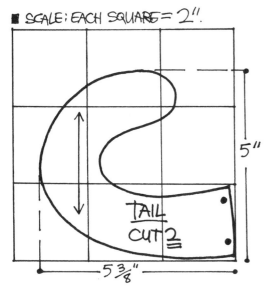

■ SCALE: EACH SQUARE = 2".

TAIL
CUT 2

5"

$5\frac{3}{8}$"

Fig. 4-75

Easy Enlargements: Use a copy machine with enlargement capability. Explain the desired scale to the operator.

How-Tos

1. **Cut the Velcro into two 3-3/4"
strips.** Edgestitch the two loop side strips to the top side of the runner as indicated on the layout (Fig. 4-76).

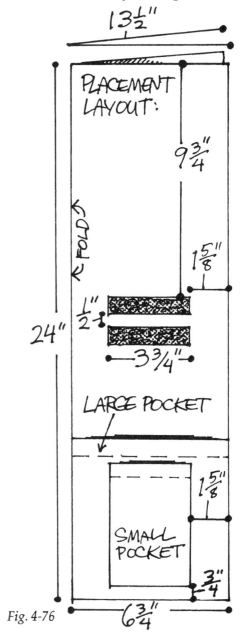

$13\frac{1}{2}$"

PLACEMENT
LAYOUT:

$9\frac{3}{4}$"

FOLD

$1\frac{5}{8}$"

24"

$\frac{1}{2}$"

$3\frac{3}{4}$"

LARGE POCKET

$1\frac{5}{8}$"

SMALL
POCKET

$\frac{3}{4}$"

Fig. 4-76

$6\frac{3}{4}$"

2. Serge-finish one shorter side of each pocket. Turn a 1" hem to the wrong side and topstitch (Figures 4-77 and 4-78).

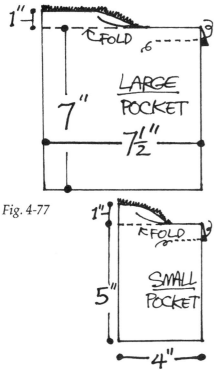

Fig. 4-77

Fig. 4-78

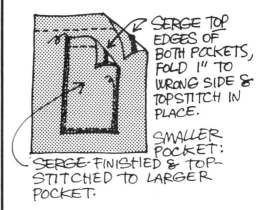

SERGE TOP EDGES OF BOTH POCKETS, FOLD 1" TO WRONG SIDE & TOPSTITCH IN PLACE.

SMALLER POCKET: SERGE-FINISHED & TOP-STITCHED TO LARGER POCKET.

Fig. 4-79

4. Fold the runner in half lengthwise, wrong sides together. Place the large pocket on one end, matching the cut

3. Serge-finish the other three sides of the small (4" by 6") pocket. Center on the large pocket, as shown, and top-stitch in place (Fig. 4-79).

edges. Serge around the entire runner, through all layers (Fig. 4-80).

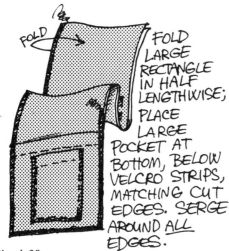

FOLD LARGE RECTANGLE IN HALF LENGTHWISE; PLACE LARGE POCKET AT BOTTOM, BELOW VELCRO STRIPS, MATCHING CUT EDGES. SERGE AROUND ALL EDGES.

Fig. 4-80

5. **Serge-seam the kitty tail pieces** right sides together, leaving the straight end open. Turn right side out and stuff firmly to within 1/2" of the opening (Fig. 4-81).

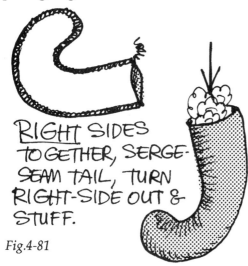

RIGHT SIDES TOGETHER, SERGE-SEAM TAIL, TURN RIGHT-SIDE OUT & STUFF.

Fig.4-81

6. **Pin the tail to one right side of the body,** as shown (Fig. 4-82).   Right

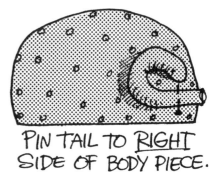

PIN TAIL TO RIGHT SIDE OF BODY PIECE.

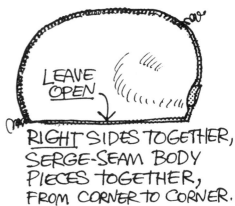

LEAVE OPEN

RIGHT SIDES TOGETHER, SERGE-SEAM BODY PIECES TOGETHER, FROM CORNER TO CORNER.

Fig. 4-82

sides together, serge-seam the body pieces, from corner to corner, leaving the lower straight edge open.

7. **Edgestitch the two hook-side Velcro strips to the right side of the**

gusset, as shown (Fig. 4-83). (The strips are spaced apart so that the kitty

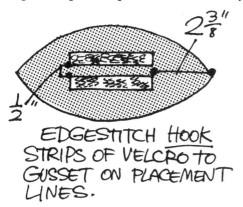

$2\frac{3}{8}''$

$\frac{1}{2}''$

EDGESTITCH HOOK STRIPS OF VELCRO TO GUSSET ON PLACEMENT LINES.

Fig. 4-83

will sit solidly, without rocking, on the runner and chair arm.)

8. Right sides together, **serge-seam the gusset to the body,** leaving a 3" opening for turning and stuffing (Fig. 4-84).

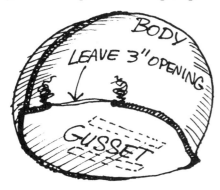

BODY

LEAVE 3" OPENING

GUSSET

RIGHT SIDES TOGETHER, SERGE-SEAM GUSSET TO BODY.

Fig. 4-84

Turn right side out, **stuff firmly,** and hand-blindstitch the opening closed.

9. **Hand-tack the tail end** to one side of the body.

10. **Embroider or paint lines on the right side of one face piece,** following the grid guide. Right sides together, **serge-seam the face pieces,** leaving a 3" opening for stuffing (Fig. 4-85).

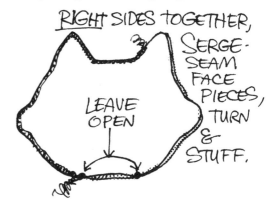

RIGHT SIDES TOGETHER, SERGE-SEAM FACE PIECES, TURN & STUFF.

LEAVE OPEN

Fig. 4-85

Turn, stuff, and hand-blindstitch the opening closed. Hand-tack the head to the body.

11. Position the runner on the chair, pocket-side out, with the Velcro on top. Position the kitty on top.

Scalloped-Edge Rose

Attach a pretty scalloped-edge rose to a hair comb or barrette to accent an outfit. This distinctive and durable edging finishes any fabric fold. Also try using the scalloped-edge for decoratively stitched hems, tucks, and crafts.

Fig. 4-86

Materials Needed
• **Fabric:** For the rose, 1/8 yard of 45"-wide red satin (or color desired). For the leaves, 1/8 yard of 45"-wide green satin.

• **Fusible transfer web:** A 4" by 8" piece of fusible transfer web (such as Wonder-Under).

• **Decorative thread:** Two cones or spools (for both loopers) of red and green (or colors desired) rayon, woolly stretch nylon, or any light- to medium-weight decorative thread; heavy thread for gathering.

• **Floral wires:** Four lightweight 12" lengths.

• **Floral tape:** A roll of 1/2"-wide, green tape.

• **Conventional sewing machine:** With blindhem-stitch capability.

Serger Settings
For medium- or heavy-weight fabric, use a wide, short (satin), and balanced 3-thread stitch. For lightweight fabrics, use a medium-width, short, and balanced 3-thread stitch. Use the decorative thread in the upper and lower loopers and all-purpose or serger thread in the needle. (The same decorative thread can be used in the needle and/or bobbin of the sewing machine.)

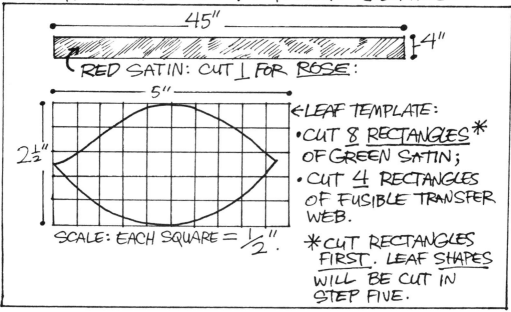

CUTTING DIRECTIONS FOR FLOWERS & LEAVES:

45"

4"

RED SATIN: CUT 1 FOR ROSE:

5"

2½"

SCALE: EACH SQUARE = ½".

←LEAF TEMPLATE:
• CUT 8 RECTANGLES *
  OF GREEN SATIN;
• CUT 4 RECTANGLES
  OF FUSIBLE TRANSFER
  WEB.
* CUT RECTANGLES
  FIRST. LEAF SHAPES
  WILL BE CUT IN
  STEP FIVE.

Fig. 4-87

Cutting Directions

Cut out one 4" by 45" rectangle of red satin for the rose, eight rectangles of green satin, and four rectangles of fusible transfer web, using the dimensions shown. (The leaf shapes themselves will be cut out in Step 5 of Scalloped-Edge Rose How-Tos below.) (Fig. 4-8)

Serge-Scallop How-Tos

1. Serge along a fabric fold (Fig. 4-88).

2. **Adjust the conventional sewing machine to the blindhem stitch.** (The

HEAVIER FABRICS— WIDE, BALANCED SATIN-STITCH.

LIGHTER FABRICS— MEDIUM BALANCED SATIN-STITCH.

PREPARATION: EDGE-FINISHING

Fig. 4-88

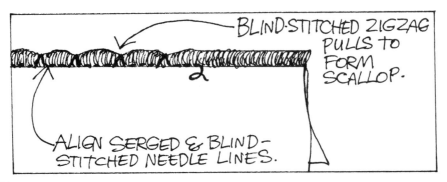

Fig. 4-89

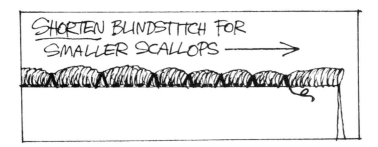

Fig. 4-90

stitch width should be the same or slightly narrower than the serged stitch width.)

3. **Blindhem-stitch the serged edge** with the serged stitching to the left of the needle (Fig. 4-89). (The zigzag of the stitch will pull in the serged edge to form a scallop.) Shorten the blindhem stitch for smaller scallops (Fig. 4-90).

Scalloped-Edge Rose How-Tos

1. **Fold the 45" by 4" satin strip in half lengthwise,** wrong sides together.

2. **Serge-finish the folded edge, tapering the ends,** as shown (Fig. 4-91).

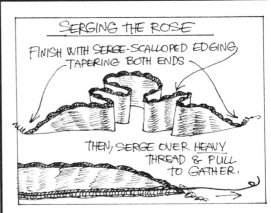

Fig. 4-91

3. Along the other long edge of the folded strip, **serge over heavy thread. Secure one end of the heavy thread and then pull to gather.** Shape into a flower and, with the heavy thread tail,

hand-sew the gathered edges together (Fig. 4-92).

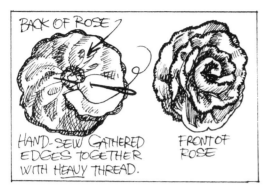

Fig. 4-92

4. **Fuse the transfer web to the wrong side of four of the leaf rectangles.** *Do not remove the paper backing.*

5. Place the fused and unfused leaf rectangles wrong sides together. **Trace and cut four sets of leaves from the leaf rectangles (totaling eight leaves),** as shown (see Fig. 4-87). Remove the paper backing from the fused leaves.

6. **Change the needle and looper threads** to those that match the leaf fabric. Also, adjust for a satin-stitch rolled edge.

7. Wrong sides together, **serge one fused leaf piece to one unfused leaf piece** along one side edge. **Then insert the wire,** as shown (Fig. 4-93), and **continue serge-finishing.** Serge as close to the wire as possible without cutting into it. Repeat for the three other leaves.

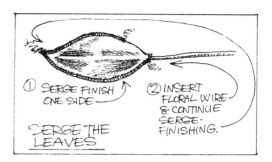

Fig. 4-93

8. **Fuse the serge-finished leaves together.**

9. Choose the three best-looking leaves and **tape the stems together** with floral tape (Fig. 4-94).

Fig. 4-94

10. **Hand-tack the back of the rose to the base of the leaves** (right above the taping). Position and shape the leaves as desired.

5. Happy Holidays!

Festive Bows

Large bows are popular for brightening the holiday season. Crinoline interfacing makes them especially bouffant and festive.

Fig. 5-1

Materials Needed

Yardage and cutting directions are for a 15" bow.

- **Fabric:** 1 yard of 45"-wide taffeta, satin, or any other decorative fabric. 1-5/8 yards will make two bows.

- **Crinoline:** 1/3 yard of 45"-wide for each bow.

Serger Settings

Use a medium to wide, medium-length, and balanced 3- or 3/4-thread stitch. Use all-purpose or serger thread in the needle(s) and loopers.

Cutting Directions

Fabric: Cut one 24" by 16" rectangle for the small bow, two 16" by 18" rectangles for the larger bow, and one 6" by 4" rectangle for the tie. (Fig. 5-2a, Fig. 5-2b, and Fig. 5-2c)

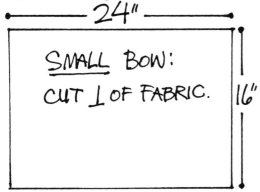

Fig. 5-2a

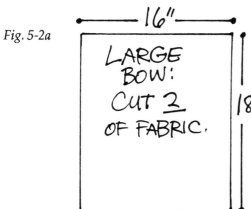

Fig. 5-2b

Fig. 5-2c

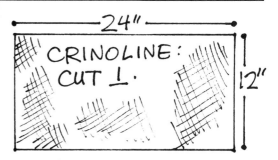

Fig. 5-2d

Crinoline: Cut one 24" by 12" rectangle for the bow. (Fig. 5-2d)

How-Tos

1. **Serge-finish** the long edges of the smaller bow.

2. **Center the crinoline** on the wrong side of the bow. On both long sides of the bow, press 2" to the wrong side, over the crinoline (Fig. 5-3).

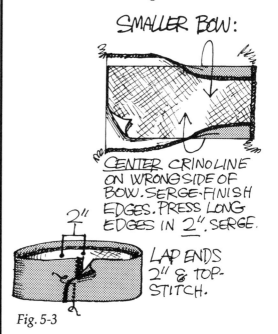

Fig. 5-3

3. **Serge-finish the bow ends.**

4. **Lap the ends 2",** forming a circle, and **topstitch** to secure.

5. With right sides together, **serge-seam the two rectangles** for the larger bow, leaving a 2" opening for turning (Fig. 5-4). Trim the corner seam allowances and turn right side out. Press carefully.

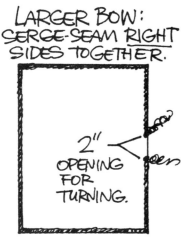

LARGER BOW:
SERGE-SEAM RIGHT
SIDES TOGETHER.

2" OPENING FOR TURNING.

Fig. 5-4

6. **Fold the tie** in half lengthwise, wrong sides together, and **serge-seam** (Fig. 5-5).

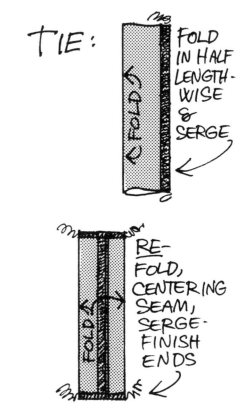

TIE:

FOLD IN HALF LENGTH-WISE & SERGE

RE-FOLD, CENTERING SEAM, SERGE-FINISH ENDS

Fig. 5-5

7. **Refold the tie,** centering the seam. **Serge-finish the ends.**

8. **Center the smaller bow over the larger bow. Wrap the tie around the bow** and hand-tack through all thicknesses (Fig. 5-6).

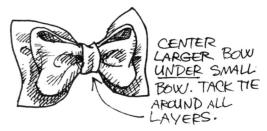

CENTER LARGER BOW UNDER SMALL BOW. TACK TIE AROUND ALL LAYERS.

Fig. 5-6

Elegant Christmas Tree Skirt

The Christmas tree skirt made from velvets and satins is elegantly hemmed with a metallic rolled-edge ruffle. Flatlocking over metallic ribbon covers the seamlines of the gored skirt.

ELEGANT TREE SKIRT IN TAFFETA, SATIN & VELVET!

Fig. 5-7

Materials Needed
• **Fabric for skirt:** 1 yard each of four 45"-wide fabrics: velvet, satin, taffeta, lace, or eyelet.

• **Fabric for ruffle:** 7/8 yard of 45"-wide lightweight fabric. One of the above fabrics may be used. *Optional:* 10 yards of 2-1/2"-wide flat lace or eyelet, or 5 yards of 2-1/2"-wide ruffled lace or eyelet may be used instead of the fabric ruffle.

• **Lining:** 3-1/4 yards of 45"-wide lightweight fabric.

• **Ribbon:** 6 yards of 1/8" to 1/4"-wide. (The width of the ribbon depends on the width of the serged stitch.)

• **Metallic thread:** Two spools for the rolled edge and flatlocking.

Serger Settings

Use a wide, medium-length, 3- or 3/4-thread stitch for serge-seaming with all-purpose or serger thread in the needle(s) and loopers. When flatlocking, adjust for the widest stitch width and medium stitch length. Use matching metallic thread in the upper looper to flatlock over the ribbon. For rolled edge finishing, adjust the serger for a narrow rolled edge and short stitch length. The metallic thread is used in the upper looper.

Cutting Directions (Fig. 5-8)

Pattern: Make a pattern for the gore using the measurements in Figure 5-8.

Fabric: Cut two gores from each fabric using the pattern.

Lining: Cut eight gores of lining using the pattern.

Fabric ruffle: Cut eight 45" by 3-1/2" strips.

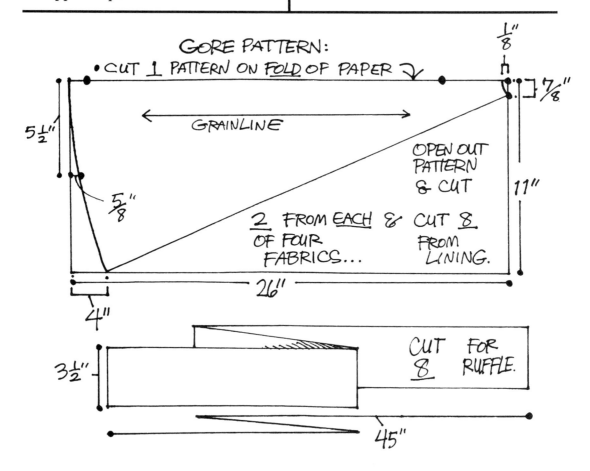

GORE PATTERN:
- CUT 1 PATTERN ON FOLD OF PAPER
$\frac{1}{8}$"
$\frac{7}{8}$"
GRAINLINE
$5\frac{1}{2}$"
$\frac{5}{8}$"
OPEN OUT PATTERN & CUT
11"
2 FROM EACH & CUT 8 OF FOUR FABRICS... FROM LINING.
26"
4"
$3\frac{1}{2}$"
CUT FOR 8 RUFFLE.
45"

Fig. 5-8

How-Tos

1. **Serge-seam the gores of the skirt,** alternating the fabrics and leaving one seam unserged, as shown (Fig. 5-9).

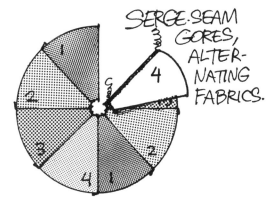

Fig. 5-9

2. **Serge-seam the eight gores of the lining,** leaving one seam unserged.

3. **Serge-seam the eight ruffle strips** together into a 360" long strip.

4. Adjust the serger for a rolled edge and, using the metallic thread in the upper looper, **serge-finish one long edge** of the ruffle strip.

5. Adjust the serger for the widest flatlock with the metallic thread in the upper looper. (To flatlock, tighten the lower looper tension and loosen the needle tension. Allow the stitches to hang over the folded edge for the flattest finished flatlocking.)

Fold each seamline of the skirt wrong sides together. Place the ribbon under the back and over the front of the presser foot (to the right of the needle and to the left of the knife) and **flatlock over the ribbon and seam.** Be careful not to catch the ribbon in the stitching or to cut the fold of the fabric. Pull the seam flat (Fig. 5-10).

Fig. 5-10

6. Adjust the serger for serge-seaming using all-purpose or serger thread. **Serge-gather the long unfinished edge** of the ruffle by tightening the needle tension and lengthening the stitch. (Fig. 5-11) (Or, set the differential feed on 2.0 if your serger has that feature.)

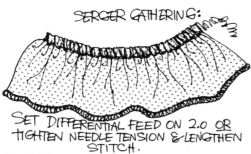

Fig. 5-11

7. With right sides together, **machine-baste the gathered edge of the ruffle** to the lower edge of the skirt.

8. With the right side of the lining to the right side of the skirt, and the ruffle sandwiched between, **serge-seam the lower edge of the skirt** (Fig. 5-12).

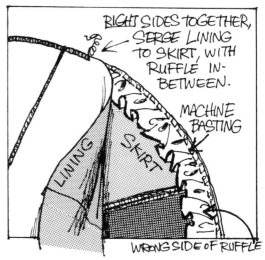

Fig. 5-12

9. Press the lining to the wrong side and match the cut edges. Adjust the serger for a rolled edge with metallic thread in the upper looper. If the fabric is too heavy to roll, adjust for a narrow width and balanced stitch. **Serge around the upper and side edges** to finish the skirt.

Serger-Lace Ornaments

Yes, with a serger, you can fabricate lace. The techniques are quick and easy and applicable to crafts and clothing. You can also use this nifty technique for shaped ornaments.

Fig. 5-13

Materials Needed

- **Chenille stems:** Twist two stems together for a longer stem. Stems can be purchases in craft stores and some fabric stores.

- **Decorative thread:** Two spools or cones (for both loopers) of buttonhole twist.

- **Ribbon:** For four ornaments, 1-5/8 yards of 1/4"- to 3/8"-wide ribbon to match or contrast.

Serger Settings

When creating the lace trim, use the widest-width, longest-length, and balanced 3-thread stitch. *Optional:* For a more delicate lace look, use lightweight serger thread in the loopers and #80 monofilament thread in the needle(s). For decorative drama, use metallic or rayon threads in the loopers.

How-Tos

1. **Serge a short thread chain and insert the chenille stem between the needle and knife.** *Serge slowly* to form a row of lace edging, being careful to keep the wire clear of the serger knives and needle.

2. **Overlap the next row,** positioning the needleline just inside the loops of the previous row. Repeat on both sides of the wire to create the lace width desired. Remember, the wire stems and edging need to be to the left of the knives as additional rows are serged (Fig. 5-14).

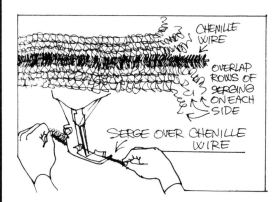

Fig. 5-14

3. **Form the lace-trimmed wire** to the shape desired. To close the shape, twist the ends together and trim. Secure the lace ends with seam sealant. Tie 5" of ribbon into a bow where the wire ends are joined.

Christmas Stocking

Cross-locked beads flatlocked to decorative trim add an elegant touch to this Christmas stocking. The stocking is then easily finished by serging.

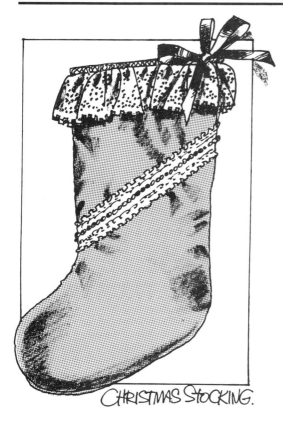

Fig. 5-15

Materials Needed
- **Fabric:** 1/2 yard of 45"-wide velvet.

- **Trim:** 3/8 yard of 1-1/2"-wide decorative flat trim. (Additional trim will be needed for testing.)

- **Cross-locked beads:** 3/8 yard of beads. (Additional beads will be needed for testing.)

- **Lace:** 1/2 yard of 2"-wide gathered lace.

- **Ribbon:** 1/2 yard of 3/8" satin or velvet ribbon.

- **Thread:** One spool of clear monofilament nylon.

Serger Settings
Use a wide, medium-length, and balanced 3-or 3/4-thread stitch for serge-seaming, and use all-purpose or serger thread in the needle(s) and loopers. For the bead application, adjust for a medium-length rolled edge and loosen the needle tension for a narrow flatlock stitch. Thread the upper looper with monofilament nylon thread and use all-purpose or serger thread in the needle and lower looper.

Cutting Directions

Cut a front and a back stocking using the grid shown (Fig. 5-16).

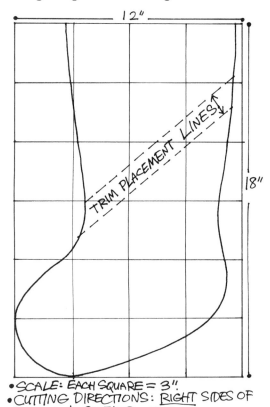

TRIM PLACEMENT LINES

12"

18"

- SCALE: EACH SQUARE = 3".
- CUTTING DIRECTIONS: RIGHT SIDES OF FABRIC TOGETHER, CUT 2.

Fig. 5-16

How-Tos

1. To make the beaded trim, fold the trim in half lengthwise with the wrong sides together. Adjust the serger for narrow rolled-edge flatlocking. (See *Serger Settings,* page 101.) Remove the presser foot if necessary. Hand-turn the flywheel to form the first stitches over just the beads (no trim underneath). After successfully serging over the beads for 1 to 2", **insert the trim underneath the beads and** *serge slowly* over both. The needle should go just inside the fold of the trim. Unfold the trim and pull it flat (Fig. 5-17).

SERGE CROSS-LOCKED BEADS OVER FOLDED TRIM, USING MONOFILAMENT NYLON THREAD.

Fig. 5-17

2. Place the beaded trim diagonally across the front of the stocking beginning 3" from the upper edge. **Topstitch or flatlock the trim to the stocking.** (If flatlocking, you will need a trim with straight edges.)

3. With right sides together, **serge-seam the two stocking pieces, starting at the upper edge** on the front of the stocking, for approximately 6" (Fig. 5-18). Open the stocking flat.

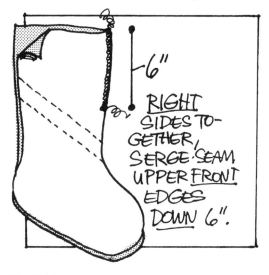

RIGHT SIDES TO- GETHER, SERGE·SEAM UPPER FRONT EDGES DOWN 6".

Fig. 5-18

4. With the wrong side of the lace to the right side of the upper edge, **serge-seam the lace to the stocking** (Fig. 5-19).

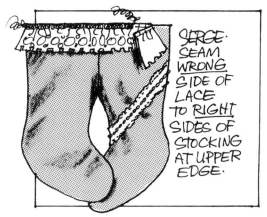

SERGE· SEAM WRONG SIDE OF LACE TO RIGHT SIDES OF STOCKING AT UPPER EDGE.

Fig. 5-19

5. Fold the stocking right sides together and **serge-seam the remainder of the stocking.** Turn right side out.

6. Cut 3" from the ribbon strip, fold in half, and **hand-tack to the inside of the back seam** for a hanger. **Tie the remaining ribbon** into a bow and hand-tack it to the outside of the stocking at the upper edge.

Poinsettia Wreath

An attention-grabber, this lush wreath is easily assembled and will provide holiday enjoyment year after year.

Fig. 5-20

Materials Needed

- **Fabric:** For the flowers, 2/3 yard of lightweight 45"-wide red fabric; for the leaves, 1/2 yard of lightweight 45"-wide green fabric.

- **Fusible transfer web:** 1-1/4 yards of Wonder-Under or other fusible transfer web with a paper backing.

- **Floral wires:** One package of at least 30 lightweight 18" lengths of wire. Cut each wire in half.

- **Floral tape:** One roll of 1/2"-wide green tape.

- **Flower stamens:** One package of stamens for the center of the flowers.

- **Embroidery hoop:** One 9" round hoop.

✎ Note: Flower supplies can be purchased at craft or some fabric stores.

Serger Settings

Use a narrow rolled edge with a short stitch length. (If the fabric does not roll easily, widen the stitch.) Use all-purpose or serger thread in the needle and loopers.

Cutting Directions

(See Step 2 below.)

How-Tos

1. **Fuse the transfer web to the wrong side of half the width of each fabric.** *Do not remove the paper backing.*

2. Fold the fused and unfused sections of each fabric wrong sides together. **Large leaf:** Trace and cut 15 sets of the green fabric and 15 sets of the red fabric using the grid in Figure 5-21.

Small leaf: Trace and cut 10 sets of the green fabric and 15 sets of the red fabric using the grid in Figure 5-21. Remove the paper backing from the fused leaves.

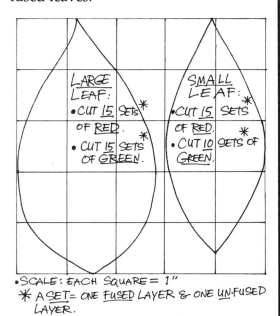

Fig. 5-21

3. With the wrong sides together, **serge one fused to one unfused leaf piece** along one side edge. **Insert the wire,** as shown (Fig. 5-22), and **con-**

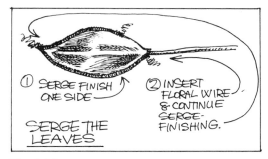

Fig. 5-22

tinue serge-finishing. Serge as close to the wire as possible without cutting

into it or hitting it with the needle. Repeat for the other leaves.

4. **Fuse each serge-finished leaf together.**

5. To make the poinsettia, wire a group of the stamen pieces tightly together. **Tape the stems of five small red leaves and the stamen group** together with the floral tape. **Tape the stems of five large red leaves to the smaller leaves,** wrapping the lower edge of the leaves together tightly (Fig. 5-23).

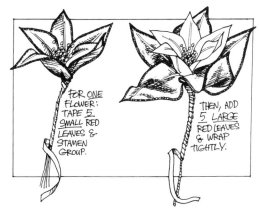

Fig. 5-23

6. Position and shape the leaves. **Wire the stem tightly to the embroidery hoop.** Repeat for the other two flowers.

7. **Wrap the stems of two of the green leaves together** and wire to the hoop to fill in the spaces between the flowers. Repeat for the other leaves. Arrange and shape the leaves and flowers. **Hang the wreath by the clasp** on the hoop.

Designer Placemats and Christmas Tree Napkins

Invest one or two hours serging and sewing these mitered placemats, copies of a designer brand sold in the finest linen departments and shops. Then combine them with these speedy double napkins to give a new twist to the holidays.

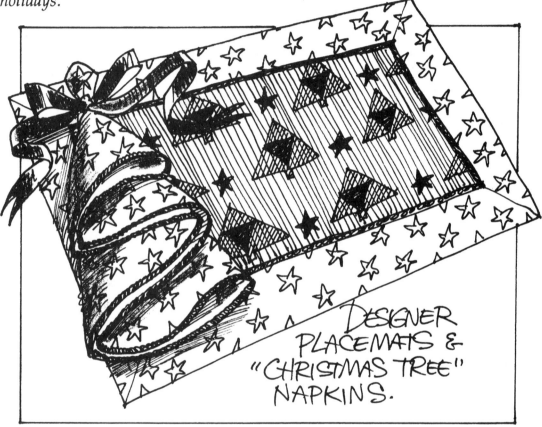

Fig. 5-24

Materials Needed

✎ **Note:** Yardage specifications vary with the number of placemats and are given for quantities of four, six and eight.

• **Fabric for placemats:** 45"-wide cotton or cotton-blend. For borders, 1 yard for four, 1-1/3 yards for six, or 1-7/8 yards for eight. For insets, 1/2 yard for four or 1 yard for six or eight. (The border and inset colors should contrast.)

• **Nonwoven fusible interfacing:** 2-2/3 yards for four, 4 yards for six, or 3-5/8 yards for eight of 22"-wide crisp medium-weight nonwoven fusible interfacing, such as Pellon ShirTailor.

• **Fusible transfer web:** 1-1/4 yards for four, 1-7/8 yards for six, or 2-1/2 yards for eight of paper-backed transfer web, such as Wonder-Under.

• **Thread:** One spool of decorative thread (for the upper looper) to match or contrast with the fabric and two spools or cones (for the lower looper and needle) of serger thread to match or contrast with the decorative thread. Wind two bobbins of the serger thread for the top and bobbin of the straight stitching.

• **Fabric for napkins:** 3/4 yard each of two contrasting fabrics of 45"-wide for four napkins, 1-1/8 yards of each fabric for six napkins, and 1-1/2 yards of each fabric for eight napkins.

• **Ribbon:** 1-5/8 yards of 1/4"-wide ribbon for four napkins, 2-1/3 yards for six napkins, and 3-1/8 yards for eight napkins.

Cutting Directions (Fig. 5-25)

• **Placemats:** Use the measurements in Figure 5-25. For the border, cut one of fabric and one of interfacing. For the inset, cut one of fabric, one of interfacing, and one of fusible transfer web.

• **Napkins:** For each napkin, cut one 15" circle of both fabrics.

Fig. 5-25

Serger Settings

• **For the placemats,** use a narrow, short, and balanced 3-thread stitch. Adjust the stitch length according to the decorative thread used; the thicker the looper thread, the longer the stitch required.

• **For the napkins,** adjust to a short rolled edge, using decorative thread in the upper looper and all-purpose or serger thread in the needle and lower looper.

Placemat How-Tos

1. **Fuse the interfacing** to the wrong sides of the corresponding border and inset pieces.

2. **Fuse the transfer web** to the wrong side of the interfaced insets. Peel away the paper backing.

3. Wrong sides together, **center the inset on the border,** as shown (Fig. 5-26). **Fuse the inset to the border.**

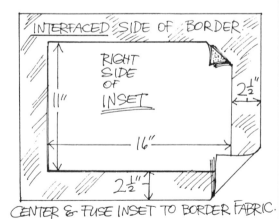

Fig. 5-26

4. On the right side of the border pieces, **serge-finish all four placemat sides.** (Don't worry about the corner threads. The corners will be mitered.)

5. **Press 2" hems in the borders** toward the insets on all sides.

6. With a washable marker, **indicate the 2" hemline corner points** (where the hemlines intersect) on each placemat.

7. **Fold the corners right sides together,** aligning the two serged edges, as shown (Fig. 5-27).

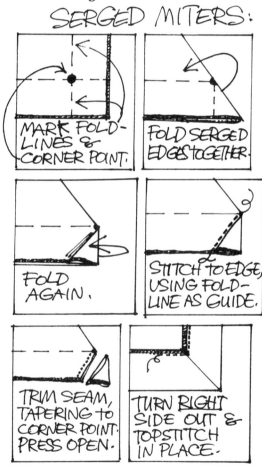

Fig. 5-27

8. **Fold the corners again,** as shown (Fig. 5-27), aligning all the serged edges.

9. Using the foldline as a guide, **straight-stitch next to (but not catching) the fold.** Backstitch at the serged edge.

10. **Trim to a 1/4" seam, tapering at the corner** to minimize bulk.

11. **Press open the trimmed seam.** Then turn right side out. Center the miter in the border corner and press again from the right side.

12. **Edgestitch close to the decorative stitching** to secure the border.

Napkin How-Tos

1. Place one napkin circle and one contrast circle wrong sides together (Fig. 5-28a). Position the layers so the grainlines are at a 45-degree angle. **Serge-finish the edges** with a narrow rolled hem.

2. Fold the finished napkin in half. Then fold again as shown to form a "Christmas tree" (Fig. 5-28b). Tie the top point with a 5" strip of ribbon.

Fig. 5-28a

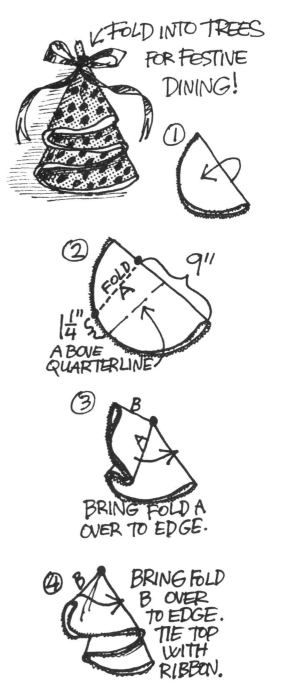

Fig. 5-28b

6. *Bon Voyage*

Earring Travel Case

This travel accessory is easily and quickly made entirely with the use of the serger—even the button.

THREAD LOOP FOR BUTTON.

←PLASTIC CANVAS FOR EARRINGS.

SERGED BUTTON.

EARRING CASE CLOSED.

Fig. 6-1

Materials Needed
- **Fabric:** 1/4 yard of double-faced quilted fabric or heavy denim, poplin, or upholstery fabric.

- **Plastic canvas:** 5" square (available in most craft/needlework departments or stores).

- **Decorative thread:** Two cones or spools of decorative thread, such as rayon, woolly nylon, or buttonhole twist.

Serger Settings
Use a narrow, short (satin), and balanced 3-thread stitch. Use decorative thread in the upper and lower loopers and all-purpose or serger thread in the needle. (Both sides of the stitch will show on the finished earring case.)

Cutting Directions

Cut a 15" by 6" rectangle from the fabric. *Optional:* Cut a 5" by 1" rectangle from the fabric (or a coordinating woven or knit) for the button. (Fig. 6-2)

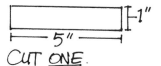

OPTIONAL: FOR BUTTON

$\vdash$—1"

—5"—

CUT ONE.

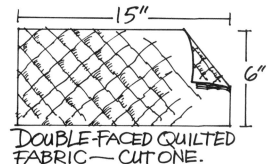

—15"—

6"

DOUBLE-FACED QUILTED FABRIC — CUT ONE.

Fig. 6-2

How-Tos

1. **Serge-finish the two short ends** of the rectangle (Fig. 6-3).

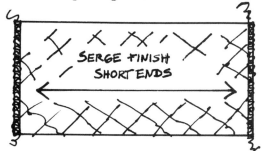

SERGE FINISH SHORT ENDS

Fig. 6-3

2. Fold one short end over 5-1/4" toward the wrong side, forming the case pocket. **Serge the long edges** to secure and finish the case (Fig. 6-4).

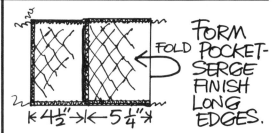

FORM POCKET- SERGE FINISH LONG EDGES.

FOLD

$\vdash$4½"$\rightarrow$|$\leftarrow$5¼"$\rightarrow$|

Fig. 6-4

3. To make a serged roll-up button from the 5" by 1" rectangle, put the right side of the fabric up, and **serge from one corner to the center of the opposite end** (Fig. 6-5). Repeat for the other side, forming a triangle. **Serge across the end.**

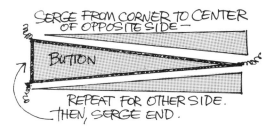

SERGE FROM CORNER TO CENTER OF OPPOSITE SIDE —

BUTTON

REPEAT FOR OTHER SIDE. THEN, SERGE END.

Fig. 6-5

4. Starting at the wide end of the triangle, roll up the button to the point at the other end. Hand-sew it to the case, as shown on the finished view (see Fig. 6--1). Make a matching thread chain andstitch a short section onto the flap, forming a loop to fit over the button.

Zipped Cosmetic Bag

Here's a fast and simple serged bag, the perfect last-minute going-away item and a necessity for travelers.

Materials Needed

- **Fabric:** 1/4 yard of double-faced quilted fabric.

- **Zipper:** One 9" or longer zipper.

Serger Settings

Use a wide, medium-length, and balanced 3- or 3/4-thread stitch. Use all-purpose or serger thread in the needle(s) and loopers.

Cutting Directions

Cut one 12" by 6" rectangle from fabric. (Fig. 6-7)

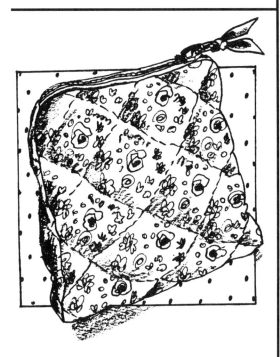

Fig. 6-6

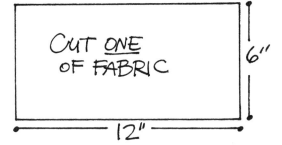

CUT ONE OF FABRIC

6"

12"

Fig. 6-7

How-Tos

1. **Place the zipper on the fabric** right sides together, **along one of the 6" sides,** as shown (Fig. 6-8). The ends of the zipper will extend beyond the fabric.

SERGE ZIPPER FACE DOWN ON RIGHT SIDE OF FABRIC, AT EDGE

Fig. 6-8

2. **Serge through the fabric and the zipper tape,** trimming 1/8" (or any excess width). Be careful not to hit the zipper teeth with the needle.

3. Place the other 6" edge of the fabric right sides together with the remaining zipper tape. **Serge through the fabric and the zipper tape** (Fig. 6-9).

SERGE REMAIN-ING ZIPPER TAPE TO OPPOSITE SIDE.

Fig. 6-9

4. **Straight-stitch the side seams,** using a 3/8" seam allowance. Then **serge-finish the seams,** stitching slowly over the zipper area (Fig. 6-10).

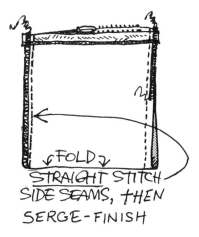

FOLD
STRAIGHT STITCH SIDE SEAMS, THEN
SERGE-FINISH

Fig. 6-10

5. **Turn right side out.** The cosmetic bag is finished. Enlarge the bag size proportionately for carrying shoes, hosiery, lingerie, or bathing suits.

Roll-Up Ironing Board

The business traveler or college student will love the convenience of a roll-up ironing board. A thoughtful gift on its own—and a real treat combined with a portable iron.

Fig. 6-11

Materials Needed
- **Fabric:** 1/2 yard of 45"-wide heavy cotton flannel.

- **Fleece:** 1/2 yard of polyester fleece.

- **Milium®:** 1/2 yard of 45"-wide Milium, a metallic coat-lining fabric that reflects heat.

- **Ribbon:** 1-1/2 yards of 5/8"-wide grosgrain ribbon.

- **Other:** Spray fabric adhesive.

Serger Settings
Use a wide, medium-length, and balanced 3- or 3/4-thread stitch. Use all-purpose or serger thread in the needle(s) and loopers.

Cutting directions (Fig. 6-12)

Fabric: Cut one 30" by 18" rectangle.

Fleece: Cut one 30" by 18" rectangle.

Milium: Cut one 30" by 18" rectangle.

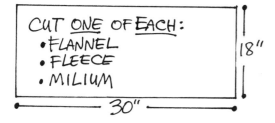

Fig. 6-12

How-Tos

1. **Layer the rectangles** of the flannel, fleece, and Milium. Secure the layers with a spray fabric adhesive, such as Pattern-Sta or No More Pins (Fig. 6-13).

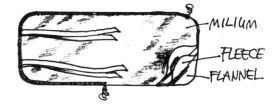

Fig. 6-13

2. **Round the corners,** using a coffee mug as a guide.

3. Cut the ribbon into two 27" strips. **Place the midpoint of each ribbon strip at one of the short ends** on the Milium side.

4. **Serge around the outer edges,** catching the two ribbon ties into the serging.

5. Roll it, tie it, and pack it.

Ultrasuede Luggage Tags

Ultrasuede® fabric has long been deemed the ultimate in synthetic suedes. Now you can treat your favorite travelers to another ultimate—Ultrasuede luggage tags. They will love the custom-made luxury and the certainty that their luggage will never be confused with another's on the airline baggage carousel.

Materials Needed

- **Fabric:** 1/8 yard Ultrasuede (or scraps).

- **Vinyl:** 1/8 yard lightweight clear vinyl (or scraps).

- **Fusible transfer web:** 1/8 yard (or scraps) of fusible web with paper backing (like Wonder-Under).

- **D-rings:** Two 3/4" size D-rings.

Serger Settings

Use a narrow, short (satin), and balanced 3-thread stitch. Use all-purpose or serger thread in the needle and loopers.

SERGED LUGGAGE TAGS

Fig. 6-14

Cutting Directions (Fig. 6-15)

Fabric: Cut two 4-1/2" by 2-1/2" pieces and one 7" by 1-1/2" piece from Ultrasuede.

Vinyl: Cut one 4-1/2" by 2-1/2" piece.

Fusible transfer web: Cut one 4-1/2" by 2-1/2" piece and one 7" by 3/4" piece.

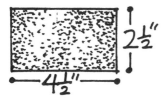

TAG: CUT 2 FROM ULTRA·SUEDE; CUT 1 FROM FUSIBLE; CUT 1 FROM VINYL

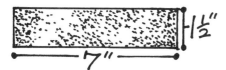

STRAP: CUT 1 FROM ULTRA-SUEDE.

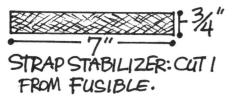

STRAP STABILIZER: CUT 1 FROM FUSIBLE.

Fig. 6-15

How-Tos

1. **Fuse the transfer web** to the wrong side of one Ultrasuede 4-1/2" by 2-1/2" rectangle. Do not peel off the transfer-web backing.

2. **Trace and cut out a business-card size window** from the fused rectangle, positioned as shown (Fig. 6-16).

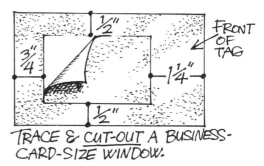

TRACE & CUT-OUT A BUSINESS-CARD-SIZE WINDOW.

Fig. 6-16

3. Peel away the transfer-web backing on the fused rectangle. **Fuse the windowed rectangle to the vinyl piece,** with the Ultrasuede side up.

4. **Round the corners of the windowed and plain Ultrasuede rectangles,** as shown (Fig. 6-17). Serge-finish each rounded end separately.

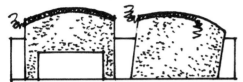

FINISH ROUNDED TOPS WITH NARROW BALANCED STITCH.

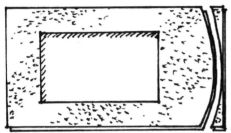

ROUND OFF TOP CORNERS ON BOTH FRONT & BACK.

Fig. 6-17

5. With the wrong sides of the rectangles together, **serge-finish the other three sides** together (Fig. 6-18).

SLIT 1/2" DOWN FROM TOP.

SERGE TOGETHER WITH NARROW BALANCED STITCH. CUT 3/4" SLIT. INSERT CARD, THEN INSERT STRAP THROUGH SLITS.

Fig. 6-18

6. **Cut a 3/4" slit through both rectangle layers** 1/2" down from the rounded top, as shown in Fig. 6-18. Slip a business card between the layers, centering it in the vinyl window.

7. **Fuse the transfer web to the wrong side of one half of the Ultrasuede strap.** Peel away the backing. Fuse the wrong sides of the strap together. **Serge around all edges** (Fig. 6-19).

8. **Fold one end of the strap over both D-rings** and straight-stitch in place. **Insert the other end of the strap through the 3/4" slit in the tag.** Thread the strap through the D-rings (Fig. 6-19).

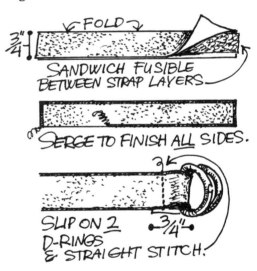

FOLD

3/4"

SANDWICH FUSIBLE BETWEEN STRAP LAYERS.

SERGE TO FINISH ALL SIDES.

SLIP ON 2 D-RINGS & STRAIGHT STITCH. 3/4"

Fig. 6-19

Carry-On Garment Bag

Keep your clothes clean and neat in this nifty carry-on bag.

CARRY-ON GARMENT BAG.

Fig. 6-20

Materials Needed

• **Fabric:** 1-7/8 yards of 45"-wide lightweight upholstery, backed drapery, or double-faced quilted fabric.

• **Zipper:** 2-1/4 yards of zipper (sold by the yard) and three zipper tabs.

• **Ribbon:** 1/2 yard of 1/4"-wide ribbon.

• **Decorative thread:** One spool or cone of rayon, woolly nylon, or buttonhole twist.

Serger Settings

Use a wide, medium-length, and balanced 3- or 3/4-thread stitch. Use all-purpose or serger thread in the needle(s) and loopers. For the decorative serge-finish, adjust to a narrow, short (satin) stitch with decorative thread in the upper looper and all-purpose or serger thread in the needle and lower looper.

Cutting Directions

Trace around a 22" plastic hanger (or a hanger of your choice) and draw the garment bag shape on a double layer of fabric (Fig. 6-21). Lengthen the bag to 50" and allow 1/2" seam allowances. Cut out the garment bag in two pieces —a front and a back. Curve out the top edges for the hanger opening. Cut one piece in half lengthwise to create a center front opening. Round the lower edges slightly, as shown (Fig. 6-21).

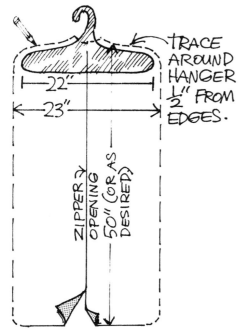

Fig. 6-21

Cut one 23" by 16" rectangle for the pocket, two 2-3/4" by 15" rectangles for the handles and one 2" by 1-3/4" rectangle for the zipper guard (Fig. 6-22).

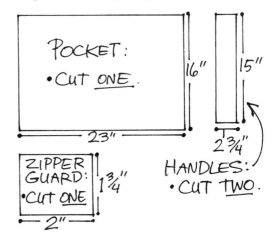

Fig. 6-22

How-Tos

1. With 1" of the zipper extending over the top of the fabric, place the zipper tape on the garment bag fabric right sides together, aligning the tape and seam edge. **With the wrong side of the zipper on top, serge the tape, trimming it and the fabric** (Fig. 6-23).

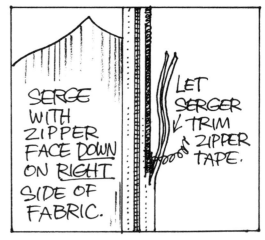

Fig. 6-23

Serge close to the zipper teeth, being careful not to hit the teeth with the needle.

2. With the right sides together, align the other side of the front with the other side of the zipper. **Serge the tape to the fabric,** trimming both layers (Fig. 6-24).

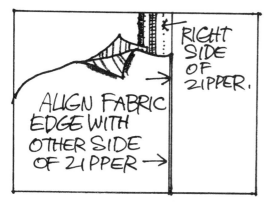

Fig. 6-24

3. **Cut the zipper** to 1" longer than the fabric. **Put the zipper tabs** onto opposite ends of the zipper.

4. Pull the zipper tabs several inches toward the center, and **make a thread bartack by zigzagging in place, with matching thread,** 1/2" from the edges of the fabric, as shown (Fig. 6-25). (To bartack, adjust for a wide zigzag stitch, at "0" length or with the feed dogs dropped.)

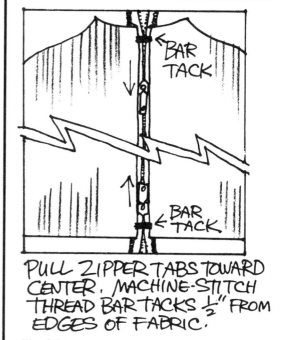

Fig. 6-25

5. Adjust the serger for serge-finishing with decorative thread in the upper looper. **Serge-finish the curved top opening edges of the bag, the right side of one long side of the pocket rectangle, and one 1-3/4" end of the zipper guard.** Serge slowly over the zipper ends at the top edge.

6. Cut the pocket into two pieces
1-1/2" from the finished edge, as
shown (Fig. 6-26). **Apply the remaining zipper to the cut edges,** using the
method in Steps 1 and 2. Attach the
zipper pull to the left and **bartack at
both ends,** as in Step 4.

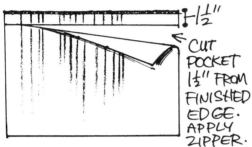

Fig. 6-26

7. On the outer side of the back, **mark
a line 27" from the lower edge.** With
the right sides together, place the
unfinished long edge of the pocket
(opposite the zipper) on this line.
**Straight-stitch the pocket to the back
piece** with a 1/2" seam allowance (Fig.
6-27).

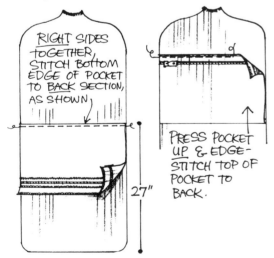

Fig. 6-27

8. Press the pocket toward the top of
the back piece. With the wrong side of
the pocket to the right side of the back,
**edgestitch through the serge-finished
edge** to secure the pocket to the back.

9. With the wrong sides together,
**press each handle rectangle in half
lengthwise.** Fold both cut edges to the
center and press. **Edgestitch on the
long edges to secure** (Fig. 6-28).

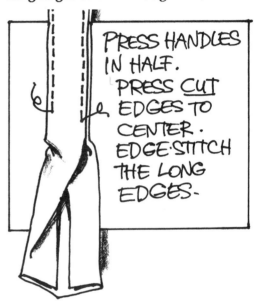

Fig. 6-28

10. To make the zipper guard for the upper edge of the zipper on the garment front, **press the 2" length of the rectangle into thirds** (Fig. 6-29).

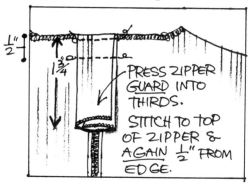

Fig. 6-29

Matching the cut edges and right sides together, **straight stitch the zipper guard to the top of the zipper** at the top edge and again 1/2" from the edge. **Fold the guard to the back and edge-stitch** to secure, as shown, making sure to catch the finished edge on the backside in the stitching.

11. Matching the cut edges, pin the handles on the upper edge and the lower edge of the front 2-1/2" on either side of the center front.

12. With the right sides together, **serge around the bag,** serging slowly over the zipper areas. **Straight-stitch from the pocket zipper to the neckline on both sides and across the zipper and handles on the bottom** (Fig. 6-30).

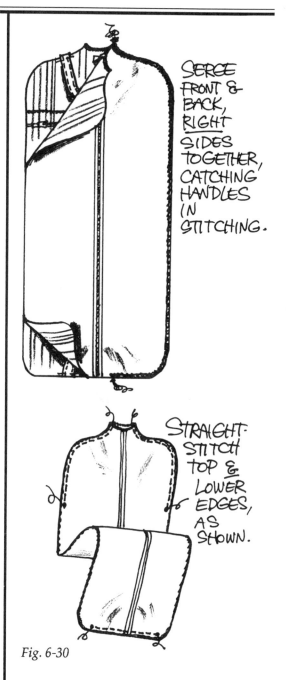

Fig. 6-30

13. **Turn the bag right side out** and press carefully. Cut the ribbon into thirds, **thread through each zipper pull,** and knot.

7. Best Wishes

Decorative Linens

Serged embellishment adds a pretty and personal touch to linens for the new household—hand or bath towels, sheets and pillowcases.

Monogrammed Towels

Make serger braid for easy, fool-proof monogramming.

Fig. 7-1

Materials Needed
- **Towels:** Purchased hand or bath towels.

- **Heavy thread:** One cone, ball, or spool of crochet thread, pearl cotton, or buttonhole twist.

- **Monofilament nylon thread:** One spool.

- *Optional:* Fusible thread.

- **Other:** Washable marking thread.

Serger Settings
Use a narrow, medium- to short-length, and balanced 3-thread stitch. Then tighten the lower looper slightly. When testing, start with a longer stitch length to avoid jamming under the presser foot. Use heavy thread in the upper looper and all-purpose or serger thread in the needle and the lower looper. *Optional:* Use fusible thread in the lower looper.

How-Tos
1. **Serge a thread chain to test the stitch length and tension** for the decorative braid. Heavier threads require a longer stitch length. The upper looper threads should wrap slightly to the underside of the stitch.

2. For filler cord, cut three or four strands of the heavy thread at least four times the length needed for the monogram. **Place the filler cord under the back of the foot and over the front of the foot, between the needle and the knife** (Fig. 7-2). Start serging,

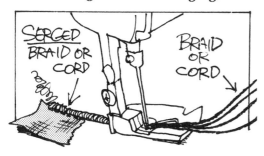

Fig. 7-2

holding the threads taut. Serge slowly. Serge enough extra braid so that you can use the best for the monogramming.

3. **Mark the design on the towel with a washable or disappearing ink marking pen.**

4. **Glue or fuse (if the fusible thread was used in the lower looper) the braid to the towel** (Fig. 7-3). For ease in fusing, use plenty of steam and fuse only a small portion of the braid at one time.

FUSE BRAID TO MARKINGS:

Fig. 7-3

5. Using monofilament nylon thread in the needle of the sewing machine, **zigzag over the braid and braid ends** to secure the monogram to the towel (Fig. 7-4).

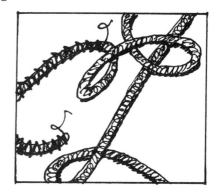

ZIGZAG IN PLACE.

Fig. 7-4

Serged-Patchwork Towels

Create a unique Ultrasuede trim with serger patchwork.

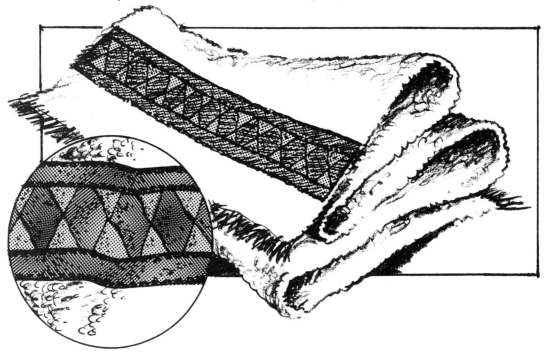

Fig. 7-5

Materials Needed
• **Towels:** Purchased hand or bath towels.

• **Ultrasuede:** Use 3" of the primary color and 2" of the contrasting color for each hand towel. For each bath towel, use 4" of the primary color and 3" of the contrasting color.

Serger Settings
Adjust to a narrow, medium-length, and balanced 3-thread stitch. Use all-purpose or serger thread in the needle and loopers.

Cutting Directions

Cut two 22-1/2" by 1-1/4" strips of both colors of Ultrasuede and two 22-1/2" by 1/2" strips of the primary color (Fig. 7-6).

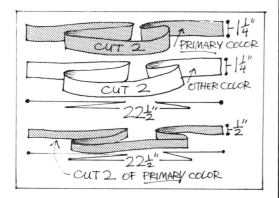

Fig. 7-6

How-Tos

1. With right sides together, **serge-seam the fabric strips lengthwise,** alternating colors (Fig. 7-7a).

Fig. 7-7a

2. **Cut into patchwork strips.** Realign the patchwork and **serge-seam** (Fig. 7-7b and c).

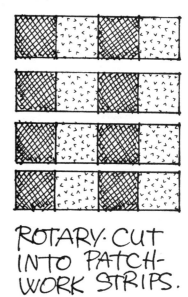

Fig. 7-7b

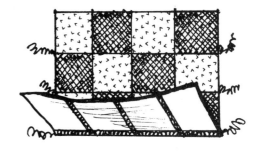

Fig. 7-7c

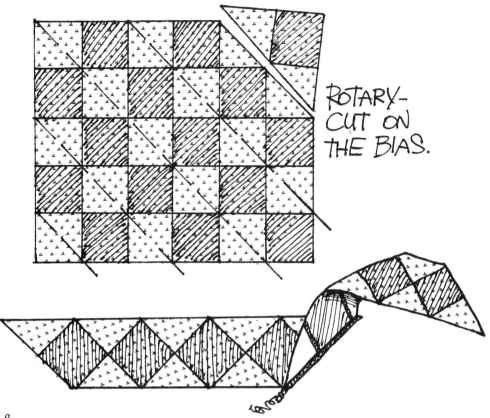

ROTARY-
CUT ON
THE BIAS.

Fig. 7-8

3. **Cut the patchwork on the bias,** always leaving the primary color whole, and serge-seam together (Fig. 7-8). Trim to fit the towel and **serge-finish the ends.** Arrange the strip on the towel, securing with a spray fabric adhesive, such as Pattern-Sta or No More Pins.

4. Serge-finish the four sides of both 1/2" strips. Place each strip over a long edge of the patchwork strip, securing with the adhesive. **Edgestitch the four edges,** making sure to catch the patchwork in the stitching.

Scalloped-Edged Bed Linens

Add this lovely decorative finish in minutes to pillowcases and sheets.

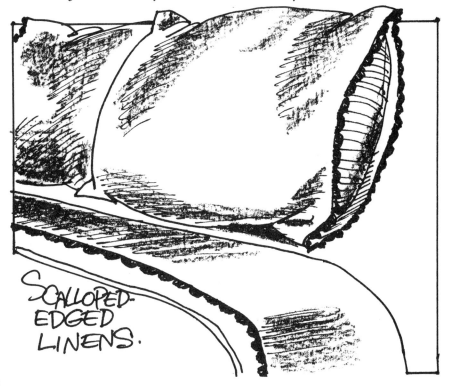

Fig. 7-9

Materials Needed

• Linens: Purchased pillowcases and sheets.

• Decorative thread: One spool of lightweight rayon.

Serger Settings

Use a narrow, short (satin) stitch length, and balanced 3-thread stitch. Use rayon thread in the upper looper and all-purpose or serger thread in the needle and lower looper.

How-Tos

For the scalloped-edge technique, refer to the *Scalloped-Edge Rose* on page 88.

Mock Hemstitched Sheets and Pillowcases

Here's another quick and simple technique to personalize linens with flair.

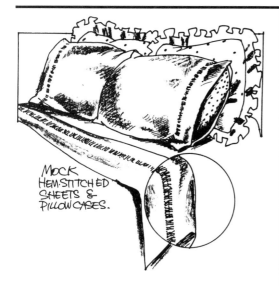

Fig. 7-10

Materials Needed

- **Linens:** Purchased sheets and pillowcases.

- **Thread:** Two cones of clear monofilament nylon thread.

Serger Settings

Use a narrow-width, short stitch length, and 3-thread flatlock stitch. Use all-purpose or serger thread in the needle and loopers. If you're using a decorative thread such as rayon, thread it in the needle.

How-Tos

1. With right sides together, fold the sheet or pillowcase along the hemline. **Flatlock the folded edge,** allowing the stitches to hang over the edge so the sheet or pillowcase can be pulled flat (Fig. 7-11a).

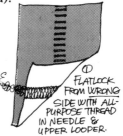

① FLATLOCK FROM WRONG SIDE WITH ALL-PURPOSE THREAD IN NEEDLE & UPPER LOOPER.

Fig. 7-11a

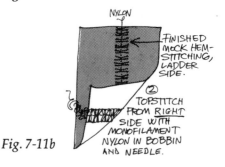

NYLON

FINISHED MOCK HEM-STITCHING, LADDER SIDE.

② TOPSTITCH FROM RIGHT SIDE WITH MONOFILAMENT NYLON IN BOBBIN AND NEEDLE.

Fig. 7-11b

2. Topstitch from the right side with monofilament nylon thread in the needle and the bobbin. (Fig. 7-11b)

Pearl-Trimmed Bride's Bag

Serge an elegant little pearl-trimmed pouch to hold keepsakes and special trinkets for her walk down the aisle.

Fig. 7-12

Materials Needed
- **Fabric and lining:** 1 yard of 45"-wide satin or taffeta.

- **Drawstring:** 2 yards of satin cord (or any smooth cord 1/8" to 1/4" in diameter).

- **Thread:** One cone of monofilament nylon.

- **Trim:** 2-1/3 yards of pearl beading.

Serger Settings
Use a narrow rolled-edge stitch. Adjust for a stitch length slightly longer than the pearl diameter. If the fabric is too heavy to roll, widen the stitch width or adjust to a balanced 3-thread stitch. Use monofilament nylon thread in the upper looper and all-purpose or serger thread in the needle and lower looper.

Cutting Directions
Cut two of each circle. (Fig. 7-13)

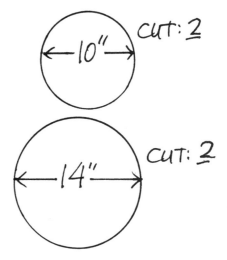

Fig. 7-13

How-Tos

1. On the right side of one 14" circle, **mark the casing lines 1-1/4" from the edge and 2" from that marking. Stitch two buttonholes** directly opposite each other within the marked casing lines. Mark the pocket stitching lines on the right side of one 10" circle. Fold the circle in eight equal sections and finger-press. Mark a 3" circle, as shown (Fig. 7-14).

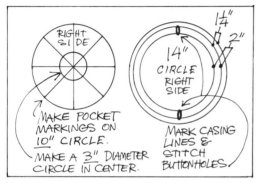

Fig. 7-14

2. Place the 14" circles wrong sides together. **Straight-stitch 1/4" from the fabric edge and along the two marked casing lines** (Fig. 7-15).

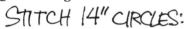

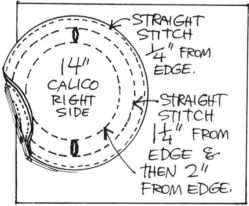

Fig. 7-15

3. Place the 10" circles wrong sides together. **Serge-finish the outer edges of both the 10" and 14" circles, serging over the pearl beading.** Remove the foot and slowly serge the trim in place, guiding it between the needle and the knife. When reaching the end, **cut the pearl strand and butt the ends** (Fig. 7-16). Seal with seam sealant. By hand, arrange the looper threads so they are hidden between the pearls. (Use a bead-trim applicator foot if one is available for your serger.)

Fig. 7-16

4. Center the 10" circle on the 14" circle (opposite side of the buttonholes), with the 10" circle markings facing up. **Straight-stitch the pie-shaped wedges and a 3" diameter circle,** as shown (Fig. 7-17).

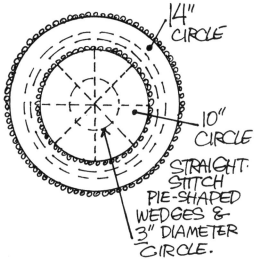

14" CIRCLE

10" CIRCLE

STRAIGHT· STITCH PIE-SHAPED WEDGES & 3" DIAMETER CIRCLE.

Fig. 7-17

5. Cut the cord into two 1-yard pieces. **Insert the cord into the casing,** as shown (Fig. 7-18). Knot the cord ends together. Pull to close.

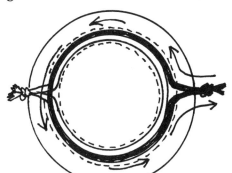

INSERT ONE CORD THROUGH A BUTTONHOLE & THREAD BACK OUT SAME HOLE. KNOT ENDS. SAME STEPS FOR REMAINING CORD IN OTHER BUTTONHOLE.

PULL CORDS TO CINCH UP POUCH.

Fig. 7-18

Lace-and-Ribbon Garter

Fashion a charming garter, finished with a serged rosette, for a quick but lovely keepsake.

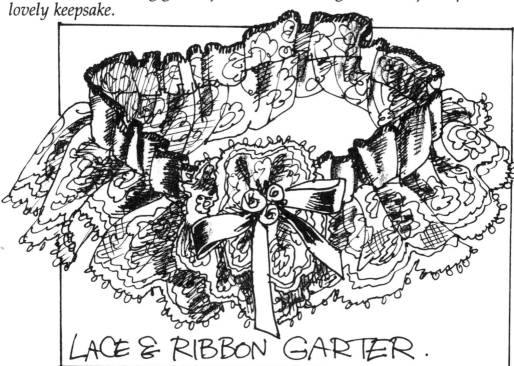

LACE & RIBBON GARTER.

Fig. 7-19

Materials Needed

- **Lace:** 1-1/4 yards of 2"-wide scalloped with one straight edge.

- **Ribbon:** 7/8 yard of 5/8"-wide satin and 1/3 yard of 1/8"- or 1/4"-wide satin.

- **Elastic:** 1/2 yard of 3/8"-wide elastic.

- **Appliqué:** One small flower.

- *Optional:* One yard of heavy thread for gathering the rosette.

Serger Settings

Use a narrow rolled edge with a short stitch length. Use all-purpose or serger thread in the needle and loopers. For serger gathering, adjust to a narrow-width, medium-length, and balanced 3-thread stitch.

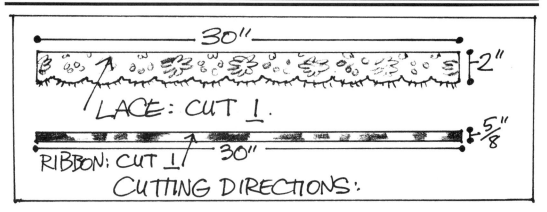

LACE: CUT 1.

RIBBON: CUT 1. 30"

30"

2"

5/8"

CUTTING DIRECTIONS:

Fig. 7-20

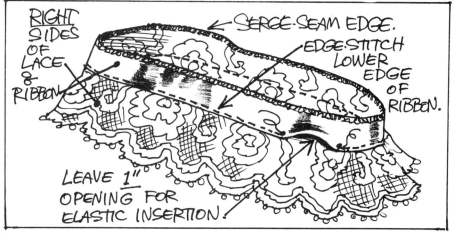

RIGHT SIDES OF LACE & RIBBON

SERGE-SEAM EDGE.

EDGE-STITCH LOWER EDGE OF RIBBON.

LEAVE 1" OPENING FOR ELASTIC INSERTION.

Fig. 7-21

Cutting Directions (Fig. 7-20)

Lace: Cut one 30" length.

Ribbon: Cut one 30" length.

Elastic: Cut the elastic to a length that fits comfortably.

How-Tos

1. With right sides together, **serge both the lace ends and the ribbon ends together** to form circles.

2. Place the wrong side of the ribbon on the upper edge of the right side of the lace, matching the seamlines. **Serge-seam the edge** (Fig. 7-21).

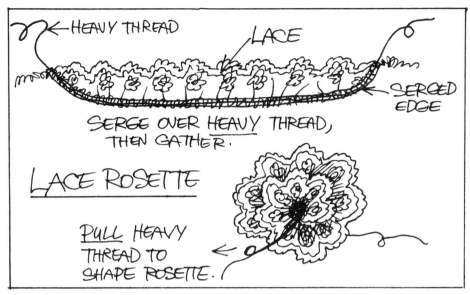

HEAVY THREAD

LACE

SERGED EDGE

SERGE OVER HEAVY THREAD, THEN GATHER.

LACE ROSETTE

PULL HEAVY THREAD TO SHAPE ROSETTE.

Fig. 7-22

3. To form the casing, **edgestitch the lower edge of the ribbon to the lace,** leaving a 1" opening (Fig. 7-21). Thread the elastic into the casing. **Overlap the ends and stitch securely.** Stitch the opening closed.

4. To make the rosette, **serge over the heavy thread, trimming 1" from the** lace and tapering to the scalloped edge on both ends. Secure one end of the heavy thread and pull to gather. If you have a differential feed, set it on 2.0, or lengthen the stitch and tighten the needle tension to gather the lower edge. Shape the lace into a rosette (Fig. 7-22).

5. **Tie the narrow ribbon into a bow** and trim ends if desired. **Hand-tack the rosette** on top of the bow.

Serge-Tucked Throw

This elegant throw is made from five fabrics in the 48" by 60" design. The quilting technique is quick and easy. Use decorative threads in the tucks and edging for a one-of-a-kind wedding gift.

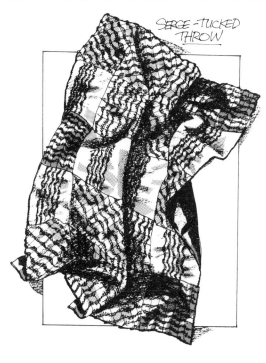

Fig. 7-23

Materials Needed

• **Fabric:** Five 45"- or 60"-width fabrics, such as satin, taffeta, and velveteen. Choose the yardage for each fabric according to the number of squares used in your design. If you're unsure how to mix and match the squares, try our pattern:

Fabric 1: 2/3 yard of 45"-wide or 60"-wide satin (for three squares).

Fabric 2: 1-1/4 yards of 45"-wide or 7/8 yard of 60"-wide taffeta (for five squares).

Fabric 3: 7/8 yard of 45"-wide or 60"-wide satin (for four squares).

Fabric 4: 1/2 yard of 45"-wide or 60"-wide taffeta (for two squares).

Fabric 5: 7/8 yard of 45"-wide or 60"-wide velvet (for six squares).

• **Backing:** 3-1/8 yards of 45"-wide or 2 yards of 60"-wide matching fabric. The backing can be one of the five fabrics used in the quilt top.

• **Polyester batting:** One 52" by 65" rectangle with 1/4" loft.

• **Decorative thread:** Two spools or cones of each thread. To add luster, use rayon or metallic varieties.

Serger Settings

Use a medium to wide stitch width, short stitch length, and balanced 3-thread stitch. Use decorative thread in the upper and lower loopers and all-purpose or serger thread in the needle. For a more dramatic effect, use contrasting colors in the loopers. For serge-seaming, adjust for a medium-length stitch and use all-purpose or serger thread in the needle and loopers.

Cutting Directions

Fabric: The quilt squares will be cut after serging the tucks.

Backing: Cut five 50" by 13" rectangles.

Polyester batting: Cut twenty 13" squares. (See Fig. 7-24.)

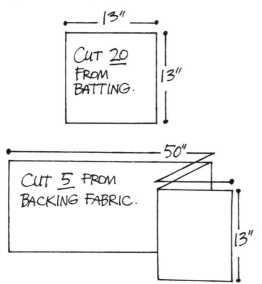

Fig. 7-24

How-Tos

1. Mark lines for the tucks parallel to the lengthwise grain 1-1/2" apart on all the pieces of the fabric. (On the velvet, we only marked five tucks to go through the center of each square, to show more of the fabric texture.) **To tuck, fold on the marked line and serge on the folded edge.** Experiment on scraps, trying different stitch widths and lengths. Serge in the same direction for each tuck to ensure uniformity

of thread color and stitch quality (the upper looper can often be differentiated from the lower looper).

2. **Serge the rows of tucks, then straight-stitch in alternating directions** 1-1/2" apart (Fig. 7-25a).

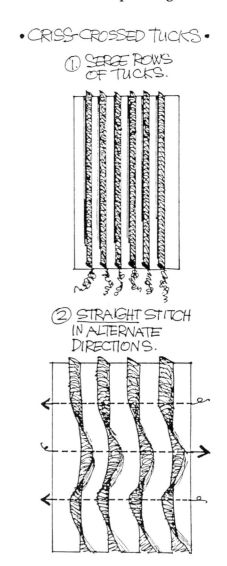

Fig. 7-25a

3. **Cut the serged fabric into 13"
squares.** (The number of squares is determined by the design.) Create a design of your own or use ours, as shown (Fig. 7-25b).

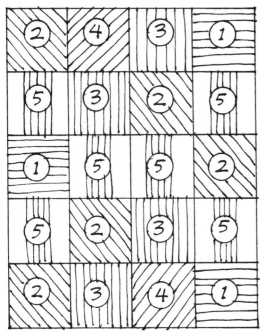

THROW PATTERN:

CUT 13" SQUARES, WITH <u>TUCKS</u> <u>RUNNING</u> <u>AS SHOWN.</u>

- CUT <u>THREE</u> OF FABRIC #1.
- CUT <u>FIVE</u> OF FABRIC #2.
- CUT <u>FOUR</u> OF FABRIC #3.
- CUT <u>TWO</u> OF FABRIC #4.
- CUT <u>SIX</u> OF FABRIC #5.

Fig. 7-25b

4. To quilt the throw, **serge-seam the batting and top squares together at the same time.** Make a quilt sandwich by placing two serged squares right sides together and a square of batting on the upper and underside, as shown (Fig. 7-26). **Serge-seam all layers on the right-hand side.**

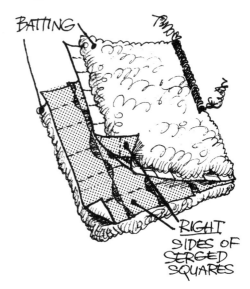

BATTING

RIGHT SIDES OF SERGED SQUARES

LAYER QUILT SQUARES RIGHT SIDES TOGETHER, WITH BATTING ON WRONG SIDES OF SQUARES — AS SHOWN — & SERGE-SEAM <u>ONE</u> SIDE.

Fig. 7-26

5. **Fold the piece right side up and repeat the process** on the right-hand square until the row is completed. Prepare the remaining four rows in this same manner.

6. Layer two backing rectangles, right sides together, under two completed rows, also with right sides together. **Serge-seam all layers together** on one long side (Fig. 7-27).

7. Fold the two rows right side out and **repeat the process for the remaining rows.** Lightly steam and machine-baste the outer edges.

8. **Serge-finish the outer edges** to complete the throw.

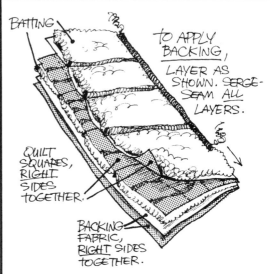

Fig. 7-27

Serger-Appliquéd Ring Pillow

A novel three-dimensional appliquéd flower holds the rings securely in style for the ceremony.

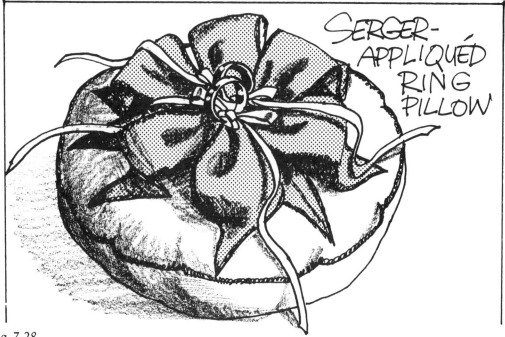

Fig. 7-28

Materials Needed

- **Fabric:** 1-1/4 yards of 45"-wide satin or taffeta (1/8 yard each for the flower and the leaves and 1 yard for the pillow).

- **Fusible transfer web:** 1/3 yard of fusible web with a paper backing, such as Wonder-Under.

- **Decorative thread:** One or two spools or cones of rayon thread for the upper looper if you're using a rolled edge, or for the upper and lower looper if you're using a balanced stitch.

- **Fiberfill:** About six ounces of fiberfill.

- **Ribbon:** 1 yard of 1/4"-wide ribbon.

Serger Settings

For the appliqué, use a narrow, short, and balanced (or rolled edge) stitch. Use decorative thread in the upper looper of a rolled stitch, or use it in both loopers of a balanced stitch.

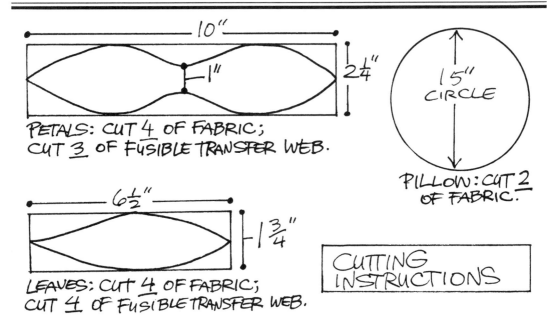

PETALS: CUT 4 OF FABRIC;
CUT 3 OF FUSIBLE TRANSFER WEB.

LEAVES: CUT 4 OF FABRIC;
CUT 4 OF FUSIBLE TRANSFER WEB.

PILLOW: CUT 2 OF FABRIC.

CUTTING INSTRUCTIONS

Fig. 7-29

Cutting Directions

Fuse the fabric and fusible transfer-web layers following the instructions in Steps 1 and 2 below. Then cut out using the leaf and petal templates. Cut out the pillow cover and form. (Fig. 7-29)

How-Tos

1. **Trace four leaves on the fusible transfer web.** Fuse the fabric to the webbing (but do not remove the backing paper yet). Then cut out the four leaves using the template in Fig. 7-29.

2. **Trace three flower petals on the fusible transfer web.** Fuse the layers as shown (Fig. 7-30), then cut them out.

3. **Fold each leaf in half lengthwise,** wrong sides together. **Serge along the**

LAYERING: FABRIC. FUSIBLE WEB. TRANSFER BACKING PAPER OR PETAL UNDERSIDE.

Fig. 7-30

fold (Fig. 7-31). Remove the transfer backing paper. (The paper that re-

FOLD LEAF IN HALF & SERGE WITH NARROW ROLLED EDGE.

Fig. 7-31

mains in the leaf fold adds body and rigidity to the simulated vein.)

4. **Serge-finish the leaf edges** one side at a time.

5. Choose the three best-looking leaves and **place them on the right side of one pillow-top circle** (Fig. 7-32). **Fuse and edgestitch to the pillow,** tucking the thread chains under each leaf to secure.

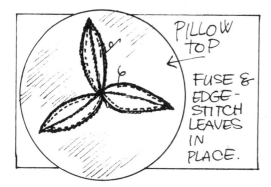

Fig. 7-32

6. **Serge-finish each petal** one side at a time. Pin a tuck in the center of each petal (Fig. 7-33).

7. **Layer the petals on the pillow top.** Edgestitch the end of each petal to the top, tucking the thread chain under so the unstitched portion will be raised three-dimensionally. **Straight-stitch to secure the petal centers to the pillow top** (Fig. 7-33).

8. Cut the ribbon into two 18" pieces. **Hand-tack the midpoint of each piece to the center of the flower** (Fig. 7-34).

9. **Serge-finish a 3/4" by 2" scrap of the fused petal fabric.** Press under 1/4" on all edges and hand tack to the flower center, over the ribbon.

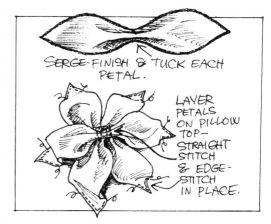

Fig. 7-33

10. **To make the pillow, serge the two circles wrong sides together, leaving a 2" opening for stuffing** (Fig. 7-35). Stuff the pillow with fiberfill and serge the opening closed.

11. Attach a ring to both ribbons and tie securely.

Fig. 7-34

Fig. 7-35

8. Blessed Event

Bath Towel Accessories

Hooded towels are indispensable for keeping babies safe from drafts or chills after a bath. Make the matching washcloths and wash mitt for a quick and easy shower gift—and one that every new mother will appreciate. Choose children's print fabric, or appliqué or paint designs on the mitt and towel.

BATH TOWEL ACCESSORIES.

Fig. 8-1

Materials Needed
- **Fabric:** 1-3/8 yards of 45"-wide fabric or 1 yard of terry cloth, terry velour, or stretch terry. (Makes one towel, one bath mitt, and four washcloths.)

- **Decorative thread:** Two spools, balls, or cones of decorative thread, such as buttonhole twist, pearl cotton, or crochet thread.

- **Ribbon:** 6" of 5/8"-wide grosgrain ribbon for the hanging loop.

Serger Settings
Use a wide, medium- to short-length, and balanced 3- or 3/4-thread stitch. Use decorative thread in the upper and lower loopers and all-purpose or serger thread in the needle(s).

Cutting Directions

Cut one 36" square, one triangle with two 12" sides, two 6" by 8" rectangles, and four 8" squares. (Fig. 8-2)

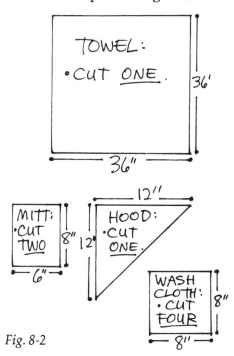

Fig. 8-2

How-Tos

1. **Serge-finish the long edge of the triangle piece.** Place the wrong side of the triangle on the right side of one corner of the 36" square. **Round the four corners,** using a saucer as a pattern, and **serge-finish the outer edges** (Fig. 8-3).

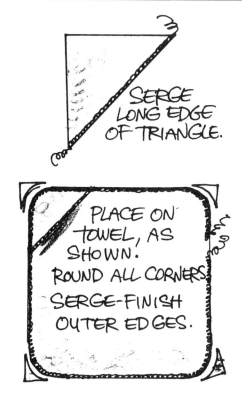

Fig. 8-3

2. To finish the 8"-square washcloths, **round corners and serge-finish the outer edges.**

3. **Serge-finish one of the 6" sides on each of the rectangles.** To make the wash mitt, place the rectangles wrong sides together. Round the corners of the unfinished narrow end. Fold the ribbon in half and match the cut edges to the outer edges on one corner. **Serge-seam the outer edges, leaving the lower finished edge for opening** (Fig. 8-4).

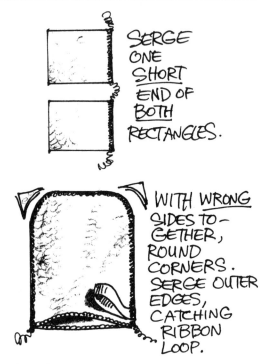

SERGE ONE SHORT END OF BOTH RECTANGLES.

WITH WRONG SIDES TOGETHER, ROUND CORNERS. SERGE OUTER EDGES, CATCHING RIBBON LOOP.

Fig. 8-4

Baby Bunting Bag

Any mother will love to wrap her newborn baby in this elegant bunting bag. Lace adds a decorative touch to this quick and easy gift.

Fig. 8-5

Materials Needed

- **Fabric:** 3/4 yard of 45"-wide bunting or quilted fabric and 3/4 yard of 45"-wide lining like flannel or lightweight fleece.

- **Lace:** 1/2 yard of 1-1/2"-wide gathered lace and 2-1/2 yards of 2"-wide gathered lace.

- **Ribbon:** 1/2 yard 5/8"-wide satin ribbon.

Serger Settings

Use a medium-width, medium-length, and balanced 3- or 3/4-thread stitch for serge-finishing and basting. Adjust to the widest width for serge-seaming. Use all-purpose or serger thread in the needle(s) and loopers.

Cutting Directions

Cut one 17" by 24" and one 17" by 18" rectangle from both the bunting and the lining fabrics. (Fig. 8-6)

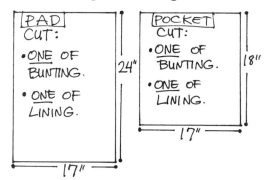

Fig. 8-6

How-Tos

1. With the wrong sides of the bunting and pocket-lining pieces together, **serge-finish one short end**. Turn the

end 2" to the lining side and **edgestitch** (Fig. 8-7).

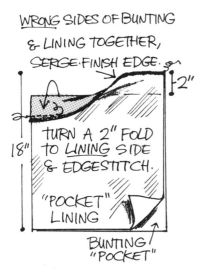

WRONG SIDES OF BUNTING & LINING TOGETHER, SERGE·FINISH EDGE.

2"

18"

TURN A 2" FOLD TO LINING SIDE & EDGESTITCH.

"POCKET" LINING

BUNTING "POCKET"

TOPSTITCH LACE TO BUNTING SIDE, AS SHOWN.

Fig. 8-7

2. **Topstitch the narrower lace over the stitching line on the right side** of the pocket with the lace pointing down. (Fig. 8-7)

"PAD" LINING

"POCKET" BUNTING

WRONG SIDES TOGETHER, LAY "PAD" LINING ON "PAD" BUNTING. LAY "POCKET" ON "PAD," MATCHING LOWER EDGES. ROUND CORNERS.

Fig. 8-8

3. With the pad lining and pad bunting wrong sides together, place the pocket on top, matching the lower cut edges (Fig. 8-8). Using a coffee mug as a pattern, **round the corners.**

4. **Serge-baste the right side of the lace to the right side of the bunting-pad piece,** as shown (Fig. 8-9). Starting at the middle of the lower edge, **fold 3/4" of one end of the lace toward the wrong side and place the right side of the lace to the right side of the bunting.** Match the cut edges and serge around the piece. Fold 3/4" of the lace end to the inside and overlap the lace folds to complete the lace application (Fig. 8-9).

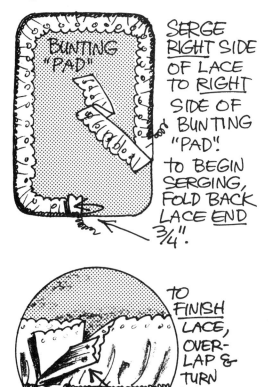

SERGE RIGHT SIDE OF LACE TO RIGHT SIDE OF BUNTING "PAD". to BEGIN SERGING, FOLD BACK LACE END 3/4".

to FINISH LACE, OVER-LAP & TURN 3/4" to INSIDE.

Fig. 8-9

5. Place the wrong side of the pocket to the right side of the pad-lining piece and align the lower edges. Place the pad-bunting piece on top with the wrong side up. **Serge-seam the outer edges over the basting stitches,** leaving a 6" opening at the bottom for turning (Fig. 8-10).

LAYER AS SHOWN:

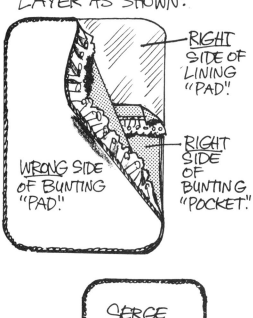

RIGHT SIDE OF LINING "PAD".

RIGHT SIDE OF BUNTING "POCKET".

WRONG SIDE OF BUNTING "PAD".

SERGE AROUND ALL EDGES, LEAVING A 6" OPENING AT BOTTOM TO TURN.

Fig. 8-10

6. Turn the bag right side out and **hand-tack the opening closed.** Tie the ribbon into a bow and attach to the lace on top of the bag.

Boo! Bear

When Boo! Bear's there, cuts and bruises are soon forgotten. Fill the bear with ice, add a hug, and watch the tears disappear. Terrific for teething babies, too!

INSTANT MEDICAL ASSISTANCE: THE BOO-BEAR ICE PACK!

Fig. 8-11

Materials Needed

• **Terry towel:** 1 fingertip size (brown or tan recommended) will yield two bears.

• **Velcro** (or any comparable hook-and-loop tape): 3" of 1/2"-wide Velcro.

• *Optional:* Scraps of washable acrylic felt (for eyes, nose/mouth, and cheeks) and fusible transfer web (like Wonder-Under). Also, 8" of 3/8"-wide ribbon for the bow tie.

Serger Settings

Use a wide, short (satin), and balanced 3-thread stitch with all-purpose or serger thread in needle and loopers.

Cutting Directions

Using the grid, cut out the front piece and the two back pieces of terry towel. (See Fig. 8-13 on page 151.)

How-Tos

1. **Center the Velcro** loop side up on the **wrong side** of the top back piece edge. Center the Velcro hook side up on the **right side** of the lower back-piece edge (Fig. 8-12).

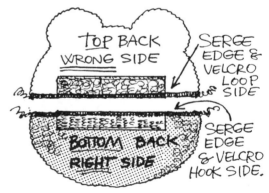

TOP BACK WRONG SIDE

SERGE EDGE & VELCRO LOOP SIDE

BOTTOM BACK RIGHT SIDE

SERGE EDGE & VELCRO HOOK SIDE.

Fig. 8-12

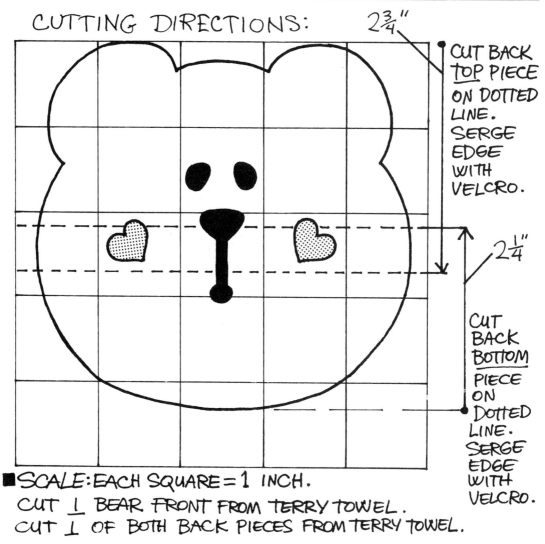

CUTTING DIRECTIONS:

2¾"

CUT BACK TOP PIECE ON DOTTED LINE. SERGE EDGE WITH VELCRO.

2¼"

CUT BACK BOTTOM PIECE ON DOTTED LINE. SERGE EDGE WITH VELCRO.

■SCALE: EACH SQUARE = 1 INCH.
CUT 1 BEAR FRONT FROM TERRY TOWEL.
CUT 1 OF BOTH BACK PIECES FROM TERRY TOWEL.

Fig. 8-13

2. **Serge to secure the Velcro pieces and finish each back opening edge.**

3. *Optional:* Cut cheeks, nose, and mouth out of felt and fusible transfer web. Fuse them to the right side of the front bear piece, matching the grid-marked placements.

4. Lap the two back pieces, aligning the corresponding Velcro strips. **Pin the backs to the front piece,** wrong sides together and **serge around the entire outer edge.**

5. Hand-tack a bow at the chin.

Instant Go-Any-where High Chair

Does someone you know need a fast, effortless way to convert any chair, any place, into a safe high chair? This soft-serged holder is completely adjustable, so it grows with the baby. A thoughtful and practical gift for disabled children, too.

Materials Needed
- **Fabric:** 1-7/8 yards of medium-weight cotton or cotton blend (pinwale corduroy or denim works well).

- Optional: 1-3/4 yards of bonded batting, such as Pellon Quilt Fleece.

Serger Settings
Use a medium-width, short (satin), and balanced 3- or 3/4-thread stitch. Use all-purpose or serger thread in the needle(s) and loopers.

Fig. 8-14

Cutting Directions

Cut two main pieces, one tie, and two tie guides from fabric using the grid and measurements shown. (Fig. 8-15)

Optional: Cut one main piece from the batting.

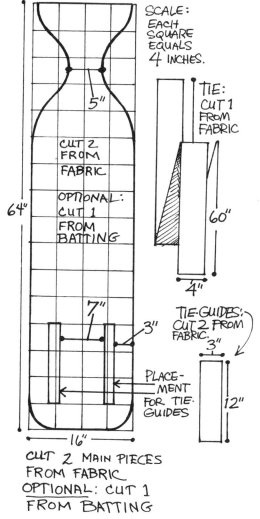

Fig. 8-15

How-Tos

1. **Place the two main pieces wrong sides together.** *Optional:* Sandwich a batting layer between the two main pieces and machine-quilt through all layers.

2. **Fold each tie guide in half lengthwise,** wrong sides together. **Serge-finish all outer edges.**

3. **Topstitch the tie guides to the main piece,** as shown (Fig. 8-16).

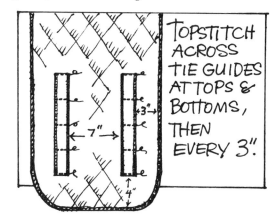

Fig. 8-16

4. **Serge-finish the outer edges of the main piece,** except for the one straight side on the top edge.

5. Fold the tie in half, lengthwise, wrong sides together, and center on the main piece, as shown (Fig. 8-17). **In one step, serge-finish the tie and serge-seam it to the main piece.**

FOLD TIE LENGTHWISE, SERGE FINISH & SEAM TO MAIN PIECE.

Fig. 8-17

✎ **Note:** Position the tie guides on the chair back. Put the main piece under the child, through the legs. Wrap the ties under the arms, to the back of the chair, through the guides (whichever slot fits the chair and the child best) and tie in the back.

Elephant Bottle Bib

This elephant bib hugs the bottle to help retain warmth. It's fun for a child to wear and fast to make.

ELEPHANT BOTTLE BIB.

Fig. 8-18

Materials Needed

• **Fabric:** 3/8 yard of 45"-wide quilted fabric and a scrap of white lightweight contrasting fabric, such as percale or muslin.

• **Ribbon:** 7/8 yard of 3/8"-wide grosgrain ribbon.

• **Elastic:** 4" of 1"-wide elastic.

• **Decorative thread:** Two spools or cones of buttonhole twist, pearl cotton, or crochet thread.

Serger Settings

Use a medium-width, short-length, and balanced 3-thread stitch. Use decorative thread in the upper and lower loopers and all-purpose or serger thread in the needle.

Cutting Directions

Pattern: Make a pattern for the bib and eyes using the grid shown in Fig. 8-19a.

Fabric: Cut two 13" by 13" squares of fabric for the bib and two 2" by 2" squares of contrasting fabric for the eyes. Then cut the bib and eyes using the patterns. (See Fig. 8-19b.)

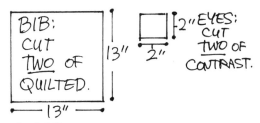

Fig. 8-19b

How-Tos

1. Place the eyes on the right side of one bib according to the placement on the grid. **Appliqué to the bib** by zig-zagging around them with a short stitch length. Draw the smaller ovals with a marking pen.

2. Place the bibs wrong sides together. Cut the 3/8" ribbon into two equal lengths and pin one to each upper corner, as shown (Fig. 8-20). Cut the elastic into two equal lengths and pin them onto the right side of the trunk.

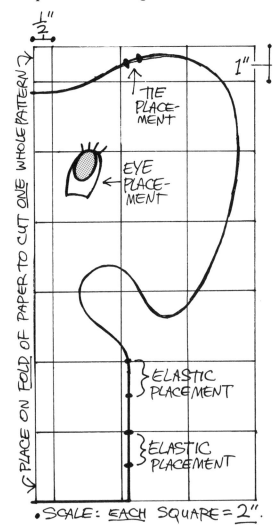

Fig. 8-19a

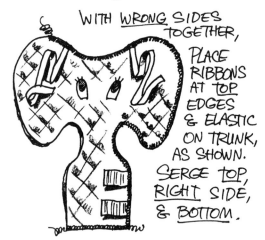

Fig. 8-20

3. **Serge-finish the upper edge of the bib,** then **serge from the upper-right-hand corner to and across the bottom,** catching the elastic in the serging (Fig. 8-20).

4. **Pull the elastic to the other side and continue serging the upper edge,** catching the elastic in the serging (Fig. 8-21).

5. Turn the trunk inside out and fold the bottom edges in half, as shown (Fig. 8-22). **Straight-stitch across the bottom** with a 3/8" seam allowance. Turn right side out.

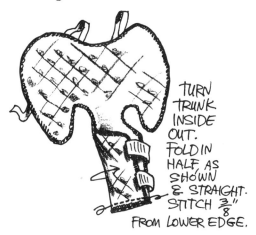

Fig. 8-22

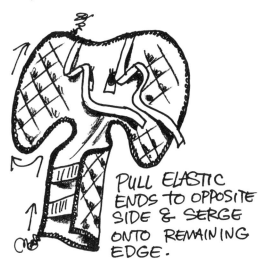

Fig. 8-21

Infant Utility Bag

This versatile and useful bag has a large outside pocket, a changing pad, and is big enough for all the necessities to keep any baby comfy and happy. The bag, pocket, and pad are lined in wipe-clean vinyl, and they close conveniently with Velcro.

Fig. 8-23

Materials Needed

- **Fabric:** 1-1/4 yards of 45"-wide fabric, or 1 yard of 60"-wide quilted fabric.

- **Vinyl:** 1 yard of 45"- or 60"-wide lightweight, soft vinyl. (Use a twin-bed-size vinyl mattress cover if vinyl yardage is not available.)

- **Velcro:** 1/2 yard of 3/4"-wide Velcro.

Serger Settings
Use a wide, medium-length, and balanced 3- or 3/4-stitch. Use all-purpose or serger thread in the needle(s) and loopers.

Cutting Directions (Fig. 8-24)

Fabric: Cut one 21" by 34" piece for the bag, one 16" by 24" piece for the changing pad, one 16" by 14" piece for the pocket, and two 24" by 5" pieces for the handles.

Vinyl: Cut one 21" by 34" piece for the bag, one 16" by 24" piece for the changing pad, and one 16" by 14" piece for the pocket.

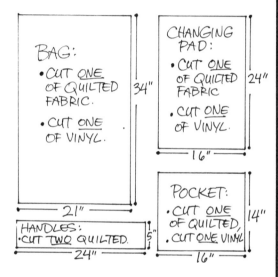

Fig. 8-24

How-Tos

1. To make the changing pad, place the 16" by 24" vinyl piece on the same-size quilted piece, right sides together. Round the corners on one end. **Serge-seam both long edges and the rounded end,** leaving the straight edge open (Fig. 8-25).

2. Turn the pad right side out and **topstitch the serged edges,** rolling the seam slightly toward the vinyl side. **Serge-finish the unfinished edge.**

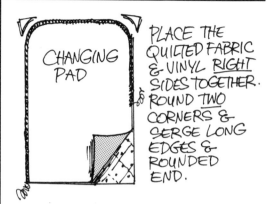

Fig. 8-25

3. On the right side of the quilted bag piece, mark a line 15-1/2" from one of the short ends. With the right sides together, place the square end of the changing pad on the marked line as shown (Fig. 8-26). **Straight-stitch the pad to the bag with a 1/4" seam allowance.**

4. Fold the bag back over the stitching and **stitch 3/8" from the fold to cover the seam and to secure** (Fig. 8-26).

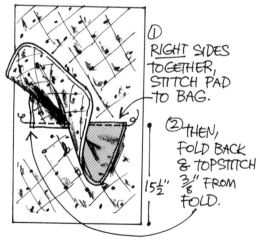

Fig. 8-26

5. With the vinyl sides together, **fold the rounded end of the pad to the seamline,** as shown (Fig. 8-27). Cut

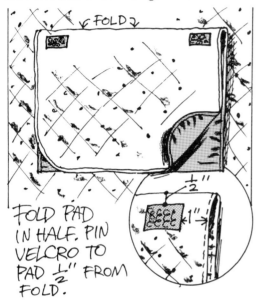

FOLD PAD
IN HALF. PIN
VELCRO TO
PAD 1/2" FROM
FOLD.

FOLD PAD UP. PIN VELCRO
ON BAG TO MATCH PAD
VELCRO PLACEMENT.

Fig. 8-27

two 1-1/2" strips of Velcro. **Pin a looped strip to each side of the pad,** as shown. Fold the pad again and match and pin the hooked strips of Velcro to the bag piece opposite the looped strips. Unfold the pad and **edgestitch the Velcro strips to the bag and pad.**

6. Place the vinyl pocket on the right side of the quilted pocket piece and round the corners on one 16" end. **Serge-seam the sides and the rounded end. Turn right side out and serge-finish the unfinished end. Turn 3" to the wrong side and topstitch.**

7. Mark a line 15-1/2" from the bag end opposite the changing pad. Place the lower edge of the pocket on the line, centering the pocket on the bag. **Topstitch in position.**

8. **Press each handle in half length-wise,** wrong sides together. Fold the cut edges into the original fold and press. **Edgestitch both long sides. Serge-finish the ends** (Fig. 8-28).

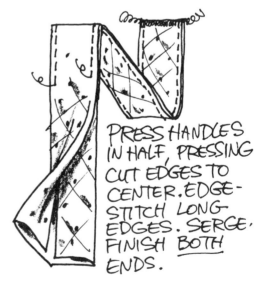

PRESS HANDLES
IN HALF, PRESSING
CUT EDGES TO
CENTER. EDGE-
STITCH LONG
EDGES. SERGE.
FINISH BOTH
ENDS.

Fig. 8-28

9. Place a handle on both sides of the bag piece, with the ends 7" apart and 5" from the upper edge, as shown (Fig. 8-29). **Topstitch each end with a 3/4" box.**

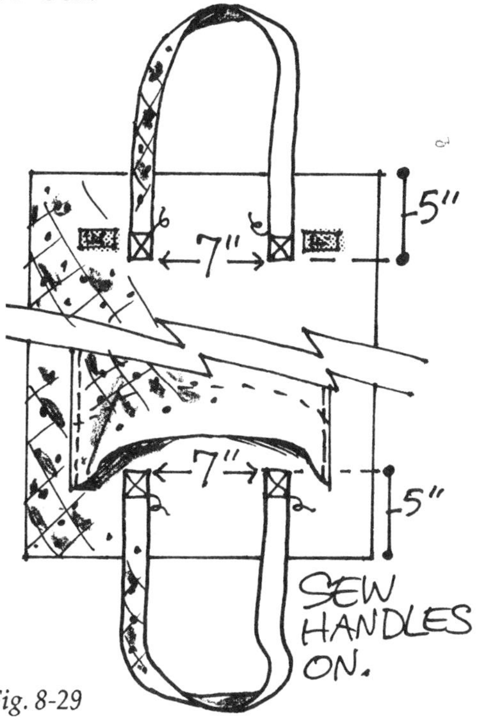

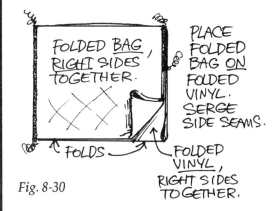

FOLDED BAG, RIGHT SIDES TOGETHER.

PLACE FOLDED BAG ON FOLDED VINYL. SERGE SIDE SEAMS.

FOLDS

FOLDED VINYL, RIGHT SIDES TOGETHER.

Fig. 8-30

SEW HANDLES ON.

Fig. 8-29

10. With the right sides together, **fold the quilted bag piece in half, matching the short ends. Repeat for the vinyl piece.** Place the folded bag on the vinyl and **serge the side seams** (Fig. 8-30).

11. **Wrap the vinyl over the quilted piece,** enclosing the seams. On the inside, refold each lower corner and **stitch a straight line 2-1/2" from the point, forming a triangle,** as shown (Fig. 8-31).

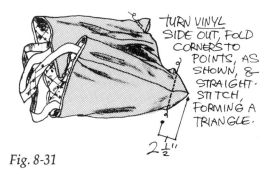

TURN VINYL SIDE OUT, FOLD CORNERS TO POINTS, AS SHOWN, & STRAIGHT-STITCH, FORMING A TRIANGLE.

$2\frac{1}{2}$"

Fig. 8-31

12. Turn the bag right side out. On the upper edge of the right side of the bag, center and pin the remaining Velcro strips. **Serge-finish the upper edge,** catching the Velcro in the stitching. **Edgestitch the lower edge of the Velcro** (Fig. 8-32).

13. Turn the top of the bag down 2" to the inside and topstitch.

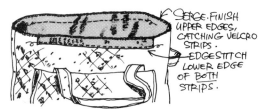

SERGE-FINISH UPPER EDGES, CATCHING VELCRO STRIPS. EDGESTITCH LOWER EDGE OF BOTH STRIPS.

Fig. 8-32

9. *Bubble Bath*

Ruffled Bath Mitt

This mitt has nylon net ruffles on one side and terry cloth on the other side. Ribbon decorates the outside, and a ribbon loop can be used for hanging the mitt to dry.

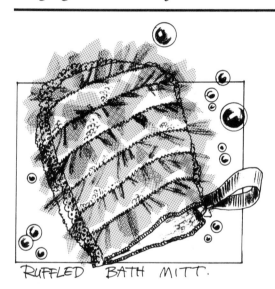

RUFFLED BATH MITT.

Fig. 9-1

Materials Needed
- **Fabric:** 1/4 yard of terry cloth or terry velour.

- **Net:** 1/3 yard of 72"-wide nylon net.

- **Lace:** 2/3 yard of 5/8"-wide gathered nylon or polyester lace.

- **Ribbon:** 1/6 yard of 5/8"-wide grosgrain ribbon.

Serger Settings
Use a wide, medium-length, and balanced 3- or 3/4-thread stitch. Use all-purpose or serger thread in the needle(s) and loopers. For serge-finishing, adjust to a short stitch length. To serge-gather, adjust for a long stitch length and tighten the needle tension. (If you have a differential feed, set it to 2.0 for gathering.)

Cutting Directions (Fig. 9-2)
Fabric: Cut two 8-1/2" by 6-1/2" rectangles.

Net: Cut eight 36" by 2-1/2" strips.

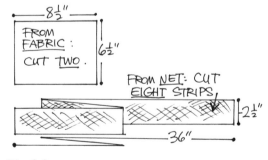

Fig. 9-2

How-Tos

1. **Serge-finish one short edge of each rectangle.** Using a coffee mug, round the corners opposite the finished edge.

2. **Serge-gather each net strip.** Place the upper edge of one gathered strip 1" above the serge-finished edge. Pull the needle thread(s) if more gathering is necessary to fit the strip to the mitt. **Topstitch the net strip to the mitt by zigzagging over the serged stitching** (Fig. 9-3a).

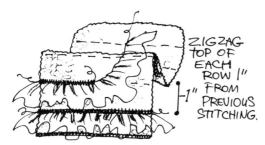

Fig. 9-3a

3. **Place the top edge of another gathered strip 1" from the previous stitching,** as shown (Fig. 9-3a). **Zigzag across the top to secure.** Repeat for the other strips until the netting meets the top of the mitt.

4. **Fold the ribbon in a loop and pin to the right side at one of the lower corners,** matching the cut edges. At one end of the lace, fold 1/2" to the wrong side and fold again. **Serge-baste the lace to the outer curved edges of the right side of the ruffled piece,** matching the cut edges and finishing the end by folding 1/2" of the lace to the wrong side twice (Fig. 9-3b). Make certain the ruffles are in position and the ends are caught in the stitching.

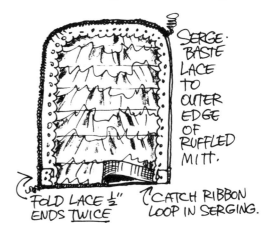

Fig. 9-3b

5. **Place the mitts right sides together and serge-seam over the previous serging.** Turn right side out.

Hanging Shelf Unit

You can quickly and easily create soft storage that's perfect for the boudoir. The shelf unit creates extra space for all kinds of storage in addition to adding a beautiful decorative touch to a bathroom.

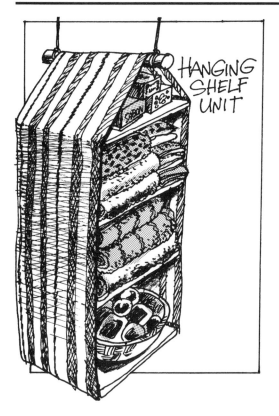

Fig. 9-4

Materials Needed

Measurements and yardages are given for a 3'-tall unit.

- **Fabric:** 4 yards of 45"- to 54"-wide medium- to heavyweight, tightly woven fabric, such as canvas, sailcloth, or outerwear nylon.

- **Dowel:** One 14"-long dowel 3/4" in diameter.

- **Cording:** 14" of rope or clothesline.

- **Hooks:** Two large heavy-duty ceiling hooks.

- **Shelving:** Three 9" by 9" shelves of foam core, hardboard, or particle board.

- *Optional:* Three 9" by 9" pieces of polyester fleece for padded shelves.

Serger Settings

Use a wide, medium-length, and balanced 3- or 3/4-thread stitch. Use all-purpose or serger thread in the needle(s) and loopers.

Cutting Directions (Fig. 9-5)

Cut two 10" by 82" pieces of fabric for the shelf wall, six 10" squares for fabric shelves, and three 12" squares for shelf covering.

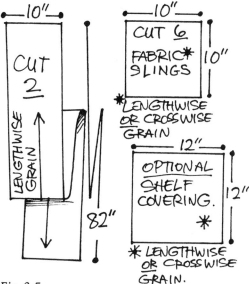

Fig. 9-5

How-Tos

1. To make the shelf wall, serge-seam the two long (82") pieces, right sides together, trimming off 1/4" as you stitch both 82" edges. Leave the 10" ends open. Turn the fabric right side out. Press, aligning the seam edges. **Topstitch 1/8" and 3/8" from the edges.**

2. To make the fabric slings, **serge-seam pairs of fabric shelves,** right sides together, trimming off 1/4" as you stitch. Leave the ends open. Turn right side out and press, aligning the seam lines along the edges. Serge-finish the raw edges on each fabric

sling. **Topstitch 1/8" and 3/8" from the seam edges on each sling** (Fig. 9-6).

SERGE·SEAM SHELVES.

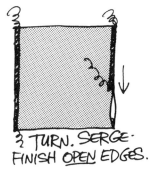

3 TURN. SERGE-FINISH OPEN EDGES.

Fig. 9-6

3. **Position the fabric shelf slings on the shelf wall,** as shown (Fig. 9-7).

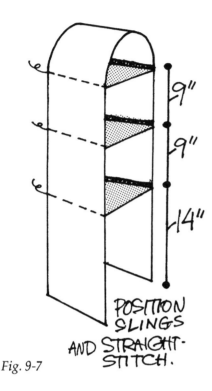

9"

9"

14"

POSITION
SLINGS
AND STRAIGHT-
STITCH.

Fig. 9-7

Straight-stitch the shelves in place 1/2" from the serge-finished edge, reinforcing with additional straight stitching to enclose the serge-finished edge, as shown (Fig. 9-8).

4. **Serge-seam the two remaining raw edges of the shelf wall together,** trimming off 1/4" from the edge. Topstitch the serged seam to one side, through all layers.

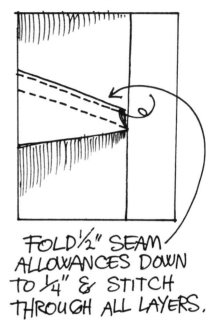

FOLD ½" SEAM
ALLOWANCES DOWN
TO ¼" & STITCH
THROUGH ALL LAYERS.

Fig. 9-8

5. To hang the shelf unit: **Place the dowel through the top opening. Tie the 14" cord to each end of the dowel, forming a loop at the top for hanging.** Hang from two large heavy-duty ceiling hooks spaced about 8" apart. Use molly bolts if you are not inserting the hooks in a ceiling joist. If the unit will be housing only lightweight objects, one strong hook may suffice.

6. Wrap the 9" by 9" shelves of foamcore, hardboard, or particle board with fabric. Staple or glue the fabric in place on the underside. Fold in the corner edges to minimize bulk, then place the shelves on the slings. *Optional:* For a padded shelf, sandwich a layer of polyester fleece between the shelf top and the wrong side of the fabric shelf covering.

Potpourri Butterfly

This 8" lace butterfly can be used to make any drawer sweet smelling. Or make two and attach ribbons to use as curtain tiebacks.

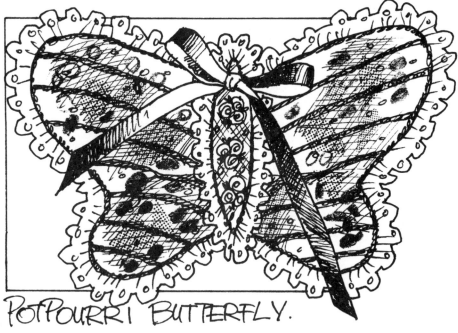

Fig. 9-9 POTPOURRI BUTTERFLY.

Materials Needed

- **Fabric:** 1/4 yard 45"-wide fine lace (so that a rolled-edge can easily be applied) and 1/4 yard of fine net or tulle.

✎ **Note:** The yardage amounts given are the correct amounts for one or two butterflies.

- **Lace:** 1 yard of 1/2"-wide ruffled lace.

- **Ribbon:** 1/2 yard of 1/4"- or 3/8"-wide ribbon. *Optional:* For butterfly tiebacks, 1 yard of 5/8"-wide ribbon for each butterfly.

- **Appliqués:** Three small floral.

- **Potpourri:** Approximately 1 ounce.

- **Other:** Water-soluble marker.

Serger Settings

Adjust to a narrow rolled-edge with a short 3-thread stitch. Use all-purpose or serger thread in the needle and loopers.

Cutting Directions

Cut two butterfly bodies, one butterfly, and one 9" square from the lace. Cut two butterflies from the net, using the grid shown. (Fig. 9-11)

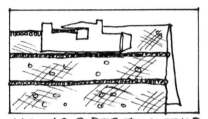

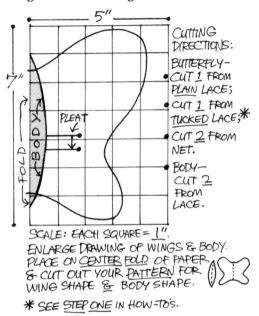

Fig. 9-10

How-Tos

1. Mark a stitching line approximately 1" from the upper edge, as shown (Fig. 9-11). **Serge on the stitching line** with the rolled-edge stitch. Using the presser foot as a guide, **serge seven additional lines.**

2. **Fold the tucked square wrong sides together,** as shown (Fig. 9-11). Stitch an angled seam, tapering from 1/2" at the top to a point at the bottom. **Cut one butterfly** from the square fabric, centering the butterfly grid over the angled seam.

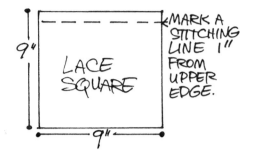

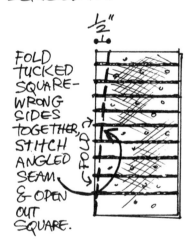

Fig. 9-11

3. With a net butterfly on the wrong side of the serged lace butterfly, **serge-finish the outer edges. Repeat for the plain lace and net butterflies.** With the wrong sides of the bodies together, **serge-finish the outer edges.**

4. With the ruffled side out, pin the right side of the narrow lace to the wrong side of the serged butterfly along the outer edges (Fig. 9-12). **With**

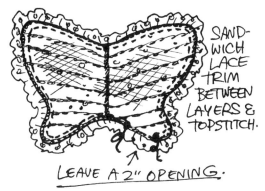

SAND-
WICH
LACE
TRIM
BETWEEN
LAYERS &
TOPSTITCH.

LEAVE A 2" OPENING.

Fig. 9-12

the wrong sides together and the lace between, topstitch the butterflies together, leaving a 2" opening. Fill the butterfly with potpourri and topstitch the opening closed.

5. Pin a small pleat in the center of the butterfly. With the ruffled side out, pin the ruffled lace to the wrong side of the body. **Topstitch the body to the right side of the butterfly** over the pleat, sandwiching the lace between (Fig. 9-13).

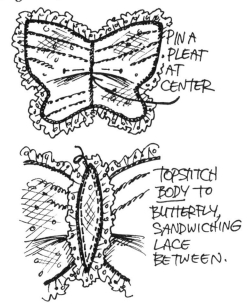

PIN A
PLEAT
AT
CENTER

TOPSTITCH
BODY TO
BUTTERFLY,
SANDWICHING
LACE
BETWEEN.

Fig. 9-13

6. **Hand-tack or glue the appliqués to the body.** Tie the ribbon into a bow and attach it to the body.

7. *Optional:* For the tiebacks, **attach the midpoint of the additional ribbon to the back of the butterfly** and tie it around the curtain.

Heirloom Hideaway Hanger

Heirloom serging decorates the satin hanger with a zipper opening to a secret compartment. A fishline trimmed ruff adds a feminine finish.

Fig. 9-14

HEIRLOOM HIDEAWAY HANGER

Materials Needed
- **Fabric:** 1/2 yard of 45"-wide satin.
- **Lace:** 1-1/4 yards of 2"-wide gathered lace.
- **Zipper:** One 22"-long zipper.
- **Ribbon:** 2/3 yard of 3/8"-wide satin.

- **Fishline:** 3 yards of clear 25-pound fishline.
- **Trims:** 2/3 yard each of desired trims and ribbon. Both long edges of the trim must be straight.
- **Decorative thread:** One spool or cone of rayon.

Serger Settings

Adjust to a narrow rolled edge with a short 3-thread stitch. Use rayon thread in the upper looper and all-purpose or serger thread in the needle and lower looper. To serge-gather, use a wide, long, and balanced 3- or 3/4-thread stitch. Use all-purpose or serger thread in the needle(s) and loopers. Tighten the needle tension(s). (Or, if you have a differential feed, set it to a 2.0 setting.) To serge-seam, use a wide, medium-length, and balanced 3- or 3/4-thread stitch.

Cutting Directions

Make a pattern by tracing around a hanger 1/2" from the edges and 9" long. Curve out at the top edge for the hanger opening. (The cover will be cut after the trim is applied.) (Fig. 9-15)

Cut one 24" by 18" piece and one 21" by 3" bias piece. (Fig. 9-16)

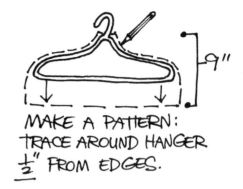

MAKE A PATTERN: TRACE AROUND HANGER ½" FROM EDGES.

Fig. 9-15

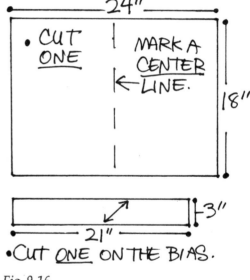

24"

CUT ONE   MARK A CENTER LINE.

18"

21"   3"

•CUT ONE ON THE BIAS.

Fig. 9-16

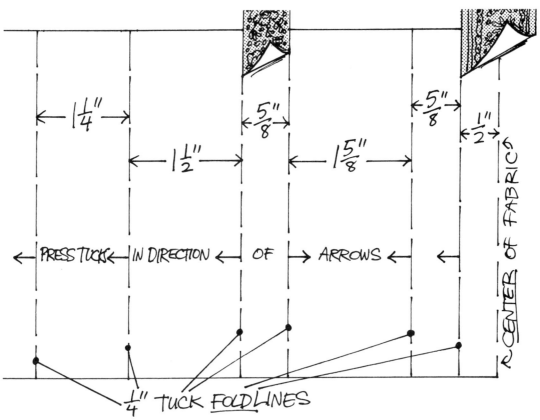

$\leftarrow 1\frac{1}{4}''\rightarrow$

$\leftarrow\frac{5}{8}''\rightarrow$

$\leftarrow\frac{5}{8}''\rightarrow$

$\leftarrow 1\frac{1}{2}''\rightarrow$

$\leftarrow 1\frac{5}{8}''\rightarrow$

$\leftarrow\frac{1}{2}''\rightarrow$

CENTER OF FABRIC

← PRESS TUCKS ← IN DIRECTION ← OF → ARROWS ←   ←

$\frac{1}{4}''$ TUCK FOLD LINES

• TUCK-PLACEMENT LINES FOR LEFT SIDE OF FABRIC; FLOP AT CENTER & MARK LINES FOR RIGHT SIDE OF FABRIC.

Fig. 9-17

How-Tos

1. Design the fabric by laying the strips of trims and ribbons on the large piece of satin (1-1/4 yards of lace will be needed later, so don't use it all here). Lightly mark the placement lines with a washable marker. Start building the design from the center and work out evenly on both sides (Fig. 9-17). **Serge with the trim or ribbon on top. Add rolled-edge tucks between the rows of trim and ribbon (Fig. 9--18).**

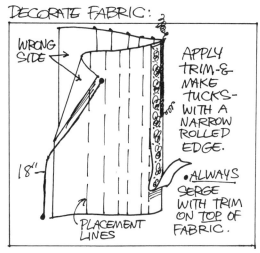

DECORATE FABRIC:

WRONG SIDE

18"

PLACEMENT LINES

APPLY TRIM-& MAKE TUCKS- WITH A NARROW ROLLED EDGE.

•ALWAYS SERGE WITH TRIM ON TOP OF FABRIC.

Fig. 9-18

2. From the decorated fabric, **cut two hanger covers. Serge-finish the curved hanger top opening edges.**

3. With the right sides together, place the zipper on the lower edge of one hanger piece, aligning the tape and seam edge, as shown (Fig. 9-19). Cen-

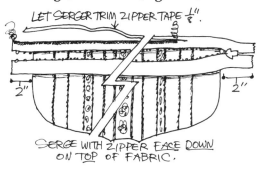

LET SERGER TRIM ZIPPER TAPE $\frac{1}{8}$".

$\frac{1}{2}$"   2"

SERGE WITH ZIPPER FACE DOWN ON TOP OF FABRIC.

Fig. 9-19

ter the zipper so the tape extends at both ends. With the zipper on top, **serge the tape, trimming it and the fabric about 1/8". Align the other hanger cover with the other side of the zipper and serge.** (Fig. 9-20).

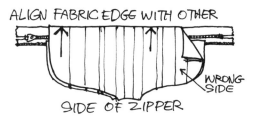

ALIGN FABRIC EDGE WITH OTHER

SIDE OF ZIPPER

WRONG SIDE

Fig. 9-20

4. With the finished edge of lace extending past the lower edge and 1/2" extending on either end, **topstitch the lace 3/8" from the zipper teeth** on the right side of the fabric (Fig. 9-21). **Repeat for the other side of the zipper.**

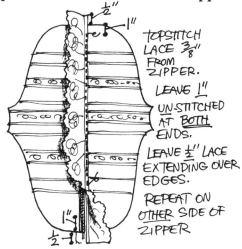

$\frac{1}{2}$"   1"

TOPSTITCH LACE $\frac{3}{8}$" FROM ZIPPER.

LEAVE 1" UN-STITCHED AT BOTH ENDS.

LEAVE $\frac{1}{2}$" LACE EXTENDING OVER EDGES.

REPEAT ON OTHER SIDE OF ZIPPER

1"

$\frac{1}{2}$

Fig. 9-21

5. Unzip the zipper halfway. With right sides together, fold the lace extensions back and **serge-seam the outer edges of the hanger. Serge slowly over the zipper area being careful not to catch the lace in the serging.**

6. Turn the cover right side out. Fold 1/2" lace extensions under and hand-tack the edges of the lace together.

7. **On the bias piece, serge-finish the two short ends.** Then adjust to a rolled edge. To avoid frayed ends, you may need to widen the stitch width. To make the fishline ruffled edge, serge over the fishline for 2" to 3", then slip the fabric underneath. Steer the fishline between the needle and the knife, being careful not to cut it (Fig. 9-22). **Stretch after serging** to create the ruffled flounce. Apply seam sealant to the edges.

Fig. 9-22

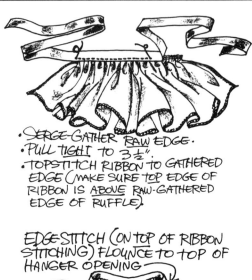

• SERGE-GATHER RAW EDGE.
• PULL TIGHT TO 3½".
• TOPSTITCH RIBBON TO GATHERED EDGE (MAKE SURE TOP EDGE OF RIBBON IS ABOVE RAW-GATHERED EDGE OF RUFFLE)

EDGESTITCH (ON TOP OF RIBBON STITCHING) FLOUNCE TO TOP OF HANGER OPENING

& TIE RIBBON INTO A BOW.

Fig. 9-23

8. **Serge-gather the unfinished edge of the bias piece.** Pull on the needle thread to gather up tight. With 12" of the ribbon extending, **topstitch the ribbon to the gathered edge,** bartacking at both ends to secure (Fig. 9-23). **Topstitch the lower edge of the ribbon (with the gathered bias attached to it) to the top hanger opening and tie the ribbon into a bow** (Fig. 9-23).

Flowered Tissue Box

This beautiful serged box is covered with taffeta and accented with chiffon or organza rolled-edge roses — the perfect accent to a charming bathroom decor.

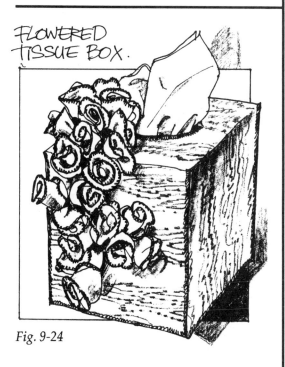

FLOWERED TISSUE BOX.

Fig. 9-24

Materials Needed

- **Fabric:** For the box cover, 1/2 yard of taffeta or satin. For the flowers, 1/4 yard each of two colors of lightweight chiffon or organza.

- **Fusible transfer web:** 1 yard of Wonder-Under or other fusible transfer web.

- **Paper:** One 16-1/2" square piece similar in weight to a file folder.

- **Floral wire:** 24 lightweight 6"-long floral wires.

- **Decorative thread:** One spool of rayon thread.

Serger Settings

Use a narrow, short, and balanced 3-thread stitch with all-purpose or serger thread in the needle and loopers. To finish the flowers, adjust for a rolled-edge setting, short (2mm) stitch length with rayon thread in the upper looper and all-purpose or serger thread in the needle and lower looper.

Cutting Directions

Cut two 16-1/2" squares of taffeta for the box. Cut six 6" by 1-1/4" and six 8" by 1-1/4" bias strips from each color of chiffon, and cut two 16-1/2" squares of fusible transfer web. (Figs. 9-25 and 9-26)

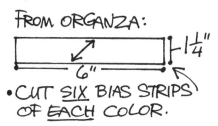

FROM ORGANZA:

1¼"

6"

• CUT SIX BIAS STRIPS OF EACH COLOR.

Fig. 9-25

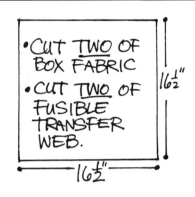

• CUT TWO OF BOX FABRIC
• CUT TWO OF FUSIBLE TRANSFER WEB.

$16\frac{1}{2}"$

$16\frac{1}{2}"$

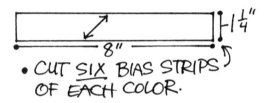

$1\frac{1}{4}"$

8"

• CUT SIX BIAS STRIPS OF EACH COLOR.

Fig. 9-26

How-Tos

1. **Fuse the layers** of fabric, fusible transfer web, and paper, as shown (Fig. 9-27).

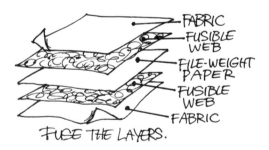

FABRIC
FUSIBLE WEB
FILE-WEIGHT PAPER
FUSIBLE WEB
FABRIC

FUSE THE LAYERS.

Fig. 9-27

2. **Cut a 16" square** from the fused layers.

3. **Cut 5-1/2" squares** at the corners

and crease along foldlines with a dull kitchen knife (Fig. 9-28).

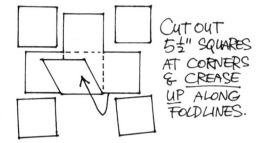

CUT OUT $5\frac{1}{2}"$ SQUARES AT CORNERS & CREASE UP ALONG FOLDLINES.

Fig. 9-28

4. In the center of one of the cutout corners, **draw and cut a 2" by 3" oval opening. With this pattern, draw and cut an opening in the center square of the box. With a satin zigzag stitch, finish the edge of the opening** (Fig. 9-29).

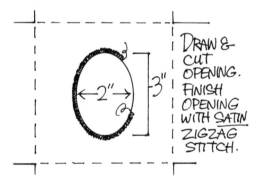

2"

3"

DRAW & CUT OPENING. FINISH OPENING WITH SATIN ZIGZAG STITCH.

Fig. 9-29

5. **Serge-finish the edges of the box.** Fold up the sides and **serge-seam the corners.** Dab seam sealant on the seam

ends and cut the threads when dry (Fig. 9-30).

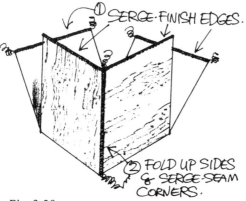

Fig. 9-30

6. Adjust the serger for the rolled-edge setting. **Serge-finish one long edge of each bias strip, tapering off at each end and serging continuously.** If the edges fray after serging, widen the stitch width (Fig. 9-31).

Fig. 9-31

7. To gather the flower, **adjust the tension for a balanced stitch** and serge over 1" of the floral wire. Then, position the wire between the needle and the knife and place the fabric under the presser foot (Fig. 9-32). Serge slowly.

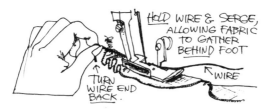

Fig. 9-32

After serging for approximately an inch, **fold 1/4" of the end of the serged wire back on itself to keep the fabric from falling off. Hold the wire and serge over the fabric, allowing the fabric to gather up behind the presser foot.** Pull the wire to the left of the needle and serge off.

8. **Straighten the folded end of the wire and bend it away from the serging. Shape into a flower by wrapping around the wire, then twist the wires to secure** (Fig. 9-33).

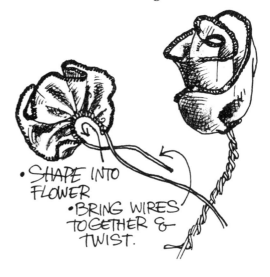

Fig. 9-33

9. **Combine the flowers as desired by twisting the wires together.** Glue or hand-tack the flowers to the box cover.

Glossary of Serging Terms

All-purpose or serger thread—All-purpose thread is most often cotton-covered polyester, wound parallel on conventional spools. Serger thread usually has the same fiber content but is lighter in weight than all-purpose thread and is cross-wound on cones or tubes so that it can feed more easily during higher-speed serger sewing.

Balanced stitch—A serge-finished edge or seam in which the upper- and lower-looper thread tensions are balanced so the threads meet at the edge of the fabric, forming loops.

Decorative thread (also decorative serging or decorative finish)—Any thread other than all-purpose or serger thread, although even a contrasting color of these is technically considered decorative. Our favorite decorative threads include woolly nylon, rayon, pearl cotton, silk, buttonhole twist, and metallic. Others are introduced regularly.

Edgestitch—A medium-length (10-12 stitches/inch) straight stitch on a conventional sewing machine, which is applied near the edge of anything being sewn. Edgestitching is often used to join two serge-finished layers.

Flatlock—A technique by which the needle thread is loose enough to flatten out on top of the fabric, forming decorative loops, when the fabric is pulled apart. The underside will show a ladder effect of double parallel stitches evenly spaced. Used for both seaming and decorative stitching on a folded edge, flatlocking lends many creative possibilities. You can flatlock with a 2-thread overedge stitch without a special adjustment; a 3-thread (and even 3/4-thread) stitch can be adjusted to flatlock as well.

Filler-cord—Crochet thread, pearl cotton, or buttonhole twist that simulates piping when serged over with a short (satin) stitch.

Heavy thread—Most often crochet thread, pearl cotton, or buttonhole twist used for serge-gathering or filler-cord in serger piping.

Long stitch—A 4-5mm serged stitch length.

Machine baste—A long (6-8 stitches/inch) straight stitch on a conventional sewing machine.

Medium-length stitch—A 2.5-3mm serged stitch length.

Medium-width stitch—A 3.5mm serged stitch width.

Narrow-width stitch—A 2-3mm serged stitch width.

Rolled edge (finish or seam)—Also called a narrow rolled edge or hem, this stitch is created by tightening the lower looper tension so that the raw edge rolls to the underside. A short stitch length creates an attractive satin-stitch edge.

Satin stitch—A stitch length short enough to allow the thread used to cover the entire fabric over which it is serged, appropriate for both a balanced stitch or a rolled edge.

Serge-finish—Most often a medium-length, medium-width, and balanced 3- or 3/4-thread stitch used to finish the edge of one layer during the construction process.

Serge-gather—Several serger techniques are possible for gathering an edge. If your serger has a differential feed, use the 2.0 setting. Another option is to tighten your needle tension and lengthen your stitch. Or, simply serge over heavy thread with a balanced stitch, being careful not to catch the heavy thread in the serging. Then, after anchoring one end, pull the heavy thread to gather the edge to any specific length. A fourth option is to loosen the needle tension, serge, and then pull up the needle thread.

Serge-seam—As in serge-finish, a medium-length, medium-width, and balanced 3- or 3/4-thread stitch, but in this case it's used to seam two layers together.

Short stitch—A 2mm serged stitch length.

Straight stitch—A medium-length (10--12 stitches/inch) straight stitch on a conventional sewing machine.

Thread chain—The joined loops formed by serging on a properly threaded machine with no fabric.

Topstitch—A conventional-machine straight stitch (10-12 stitches/inch) used to attach one layer (often serged-finished) to another. Topstitching sometimes becomes a decorative design detail.

Very wide stitch—A 7.5mm serged stitch width, available only on some serger models.

Wide stitch—A 5mm serged stitch width.

Woolly nylon—One of our favorite decorative threads that has become popular with the advent of serger sewing. A crimped nylon thread, it fluffs out to fill in any see-through spaces caused by a less-than-perfect decorative edge.

Zigzag stitch—A basic stitch on a conventional sewing machine that forms a back-and-forth pattern similar to herringbone.

Index

About the Authors

Naomi Baker is a nationally recognized serger authority, who contributes monthly to *Update* newsletters and has authored several *Update* booklets. A Home Economics graduate of Iowa State University, Naomi worked for Stretch & Sew for 10 years. She also has been an instructor for the Palmer/Pletsch Serger Workshops and has provided extensive research for their publications on serging. Naomi specializes in technique research and development and is well-known for her dressmaking skills.

Naomi has a sewing consulting and dressmaking business that serves several companies in the homesewing industry. She lives and works in Springfield, Oregon, with her husband, three children, dog, huge fabric stash and an enviable number of sergers and sewing machines.

Tammy Young has combined creativity and practicality in her writing and publishing career. Having worked for several years in the ready-to-wear fashion industry, she is known for her ability to translate retail trends into homesewing techniques. Tammy is a Home Economics graduate of Oregon State University and a former extension agent and high school home economics teacher.

Her office and home are located in downtown San Francisco, where she publishes *Update* newsletters and booklets, overseeing all facets of the business, including editing, illustration, layout, printing, and managing all other business details. When her hectic schedule allows, Tammy travels stateside and abroad, frequently picking up fashion and fabric trends for her publications.